Sentences

Name _____

> A sentence is a group of words which expres[s] [a] thought.

Write **S** before each group of words that is a **sentence**. Write **N** befor[e] [each] group of words that is **not** a sentence.

____ 1. People admire the work of Orville and Wilbur Wright.

____ 2. They worked in the field of aviation.

____ 3. To try the airplane.

____ 4. The wind across the sand.

____ 5. December 14, 1903 was a cold day.

____ 6. Wilbur was the first to try the plane.

____ 7. It stayed in the air just 2½ seconds.

____ 8. This unsuccessful flight.

____ 9. Three days later, Orville flew the plane.

____ 10. It flew 120 feet in 12 seconds.

____ 11. The two brothers were happy with this flight.

____ 12. On the same day, December 17th.

____ 13. Orville made another flight, and Wilbur made two.

____ 14. The longest flight lasted 59 seconds.

____ 15. Flew 852 feet.

____ 16. These early flights were just the beginning.

____ 17. Spent four years preparing.

____ 18. Orville and Wilbur Wright were serious about flying.

____ 19. Confident of their hard work.

____ 20. They would be amazed with the progress in aviation.

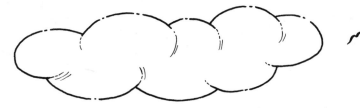

A sentence is a group of words which express a complete thought.

Write **S** in the blank if it is a complete thought and **NS** if it is not a complete thought.

____ 1. A greenhouse is a building.
____ 2. Mostly glass windows and a glass roof.
____ 3. The lighting in the greenhouse.
____ 4. The building is not green.
____ 5. It is colorless.
____ 6. Many green things in the greenhouse.
____ 7. The glass protects the plants.
____ 8. In winter a greenhouse is heated.
____ 9. Much care is needed for the plants.
____ 10. Plants are cared for each day.
____ 11. Bugs are sometimes a problem.
____ 12. Greenhouse with many different areas.
____ 13. Spray all plants twice a year.
____ 14. Plants can be grown during any season.
____ 15. Many families in the north.
____ 16. Some vegetables by the door.
____ 17. You can harvest vegetables in a greenhouse.
____ 18. When spring comes plants may be removed.
____ 19. Watch them grow.
____ 20. Come visit our greenhouse.

On another sheet of paper, rewrite the incomplete thoughts as sentences.

Subject of the Sentence

> The subject is that part of a sentence that names a person, a place or a thing about which a statement is made. It may be a noun or pronoun.

Underline the subject in the following sentences.

This <u>report</u> is about Central America.

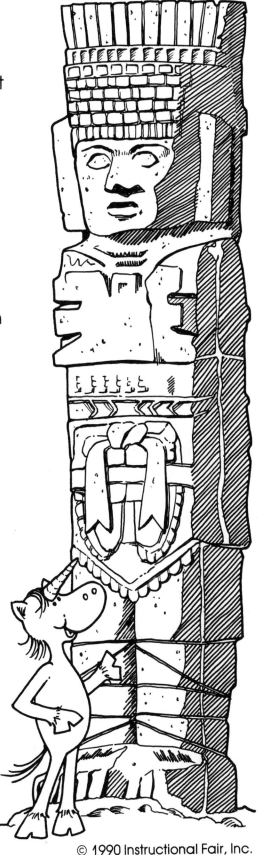

1. Central America is a narrow stretch of land that connects North America and South America.
2. It is part of the North American continent.
3. There are six small countries which make up Central America.
4. Central America is not as large as the state of Texas.
5. The countries that make up Central America are Honduras, Nicaragua, Guatemala, El Salvador, Costa Rica and Panama.
6. British Honduras is also part of Central America.
7. The United States Panama Canal Zone is also in this area.
8. The people of Central America belong to a variety of different groups.
9. In earliest times there were many different tribes.
10. The tribes were different in language, appearance and way of living.
11. The Mayas were the most important.
12. They built great cities on the plains in Guatemala.
13. The Mayas built temples that looked like the pyramids in Egypt.
14. The Aztec Indians from Mexico had a great civilization.
15. The Spaniards began to settle in Central America about four hundred years ago.
16. They came in large numbers.
17. Most people in Central America are Roman Catholic.
18. They speak Spanish but learn English in school.
19. Central America is mostly made up of high mountains.
20. The people live in the high areas because it's always like spring.

3

The Complete Subject

> The person, the place or thing about which a statement is made is called the simple subject or the subject. A simple subject with all its modifiers is called the complete subject.

Underline the complete subject.

<u>People from many states</u> visit the St. Louis Zoo.

1. The St. Louis Zoo is a great place to visit.
2. The circus seals perform daily.
3. The people in the arena cheered.
4. A trained juggler entertained us.
5. The furry baby bear jumped out of his basket.
6. The frightened little lion ran by his mother.
7. The tall giraffes ate leaves from tree tops.
8. A vivacious monkey danced to some disco music.
9. Enormous elephants held on to each other.
10. The brightly-colored peacock opened his feathers.
11. Animals were fed at feeding time.
12. The llama came to the zoo from South America.
13. Tall weeds grew over part of the zoo until the goats took charge.
14. My teacher told us the giraffes gallop very fast.
15. The black and white penguins looked like they had on tuxedos.
16. Mary and I visited Big Cat Country.
17. The long, thick snakes gave me a eerie feeling.
18. The old grizzly bear was taking a nap.
19. The 1904 Bird House was an exciting exhibit.
20. My day at the zoo was terrific.

Predicate of the Sentence

> The predicate is that part of a sentence that tells something about the subject. All sentences must contain a predicate which is always a verb. The most important part of any sentence is the predicate.

Circle the predicate in each sentence.

A trip to British Columbia (is) a great experience.

1. British Columbia is the western-most province in Canada.
2. Early settlers came from Great Britain.
3. Most people of today are Canadian-born.
4. The people work in a variety of industries.
5. They work in sawmills, fish canneries and wood factories.
6. The lumberjacks cut wood in the great northern forests.
7. Many people farm the land.
8. British Columbia ranks third in the production of copper, gold and coal.
9. The Anglican church is the largest in British Columbia.
10. British Columbia is extremely mountainous.
11. British Columbia has a warmer climate than the other Canadian provinces.
12. Captain James Cook landed on Vancouver Island more than 175 years ago.
13. They exchanged goods for furs.
14. Gold was discovered in this area in 1858.
15. Today British Columbia ships products all over the world.
16. It was difficult to build a railroad because of the high mountains.
17. Trade flourished and cities grew rapidly.
18. The lumber industry grew rapidly.
19. The water route from Vancouver to Alaska is one of the most beautiful trips in the world.
20. There are many attractions to visit in British Columbia.

> The simple predicate with all its modifiers is called the complete predicate.

Underline the complete predicate.

The study of ancient Greece <u>would be interesting.</u>

1. Did you know the ancient Greeks wrote many plays?
2. The history of Greece goes back for thousands of years.
3. The earliest record shows the beginning of Greece in 776 B.C.
4. The Greek civilization came to its climax in 450 B.C.
5. The expanding Roman Empire overshadowed Greece.
6. The ancient Greeks did not have a single government.
7. They lived in separate city-states.
8. Early Greeks lived in low houses.
9. The public buildings in a Greek city were most beautiful.
10. Most of the public buildings were temples to gods.
11. The Greeks worshiped many gods.
12. The Greeks built the first open-air theater.
13. All of the characters were played by men.
14. The Greeks loved athletics.
15. The best athletes would meet every four years in Olympia.
16. Ancient Greece was the center of science.
17. Many early Greeks gave much wisdom to the world.
18. In ancient Greece, many wars were fought between the city-states.
19. The Greeks taught the Romans much about art and literature.
20. The history of ancient Greece was ended in 1453.

Compound Predicates

A sentence may have a compound predicate. A conjunction connects the compound predicate of a sentence.

Underline the compound predicate and circle the conjunction which connects them.

You <u>read</u> (and) <u>remember</u> your homework.

1. We will read and study about insects.
2. Insects live and reproduce nearly all over the world.
3. Many insects live and die within a relatively short period of time.
4. Some insects develop and grow in four stages.
5. Other insects hatch and emerge from their eggs looking like the adult insects.
6. Some insects grow and shed their skins several times during their life cycles.
7. Some types of insects live and work in big insect societies.
8. Experts identified and labeled the three body parts of insects.
9. All insects have and use six legs and one pair of feelers.
10. Some insects crawl and hop.
11. Other insects jump or walk.
12. Most insects walk or fly.
13. Many insects possess and use wings as their chief means of movement.
14. Some can fly and glide through the air for considerable distances.
15. Most insects inhale and exhale air.
16. Tiny tubes receive and send air to all parts of their bodies.
17. Air enters and reaches the tubes through tiny holes called spiracles.
18. Scientists classified and grouped the hundreds of thousands of insects into various orders.

Subject and Predicate

> The subject is the part of the sentence that tells the person, place or thing about which the statement is made.
> The predicate is the part of the sentence that tells something about the subject.

Circle the subject and underline the verb in each sentence.

1. Charlotte Bronte wrote the book, Jane Eyre.
2. Emily Bronte wrote the book, Wuthering Heights.
3. The two sisters lived in Yorkshire, England.
4. These girls suffered tragedies and poor health.
5. The sisters wrote stories as a relief from their problems.
6. Charlotte wrote Jane Eyre from a woman's point of view.
7. The book broke with traditional writing.
8. The heroine of the story was a realistic character.
9. The book grew in appreciation through the years.
10. Emily Bronte polished her writing ability.
11. This writer placed her deep feelings in the characters of her story.
12. Emily was a shy girl.
13. The girl avoided people outside her own family.
14. Writing was an outlet for Charlotte and Emily Bronte.
15. The sisters became famous.
16. Their two books are masterpieces.
17. Many people read their books.
18. The novels hold a high place in literature.

8

Review on Complete Subject and Complete Predicate

Name _____

Underline the Complete Subject with one line and the Complete Predicate with two lines.

The country of Germany is very old.

1. Germany is a country in central Europe.
2. The people of Germany speak the German language.
3. At one time Germany was a single country.
4. In 1939, when World War II began, Germany was the richest country in Europe.
5. It was also the most powerful.
6. The German people called this country Deutschland.
7. Most of the people in Germany descended from Germanic tribes.
8. The Germans who live in Northern Germany are mainly Protestants.
9. Those who live in the southern part are mostly Roman Catholics.
10. The main Protestant religion is Lutheran founded by a German, Martin Luther.
11. German people are extremely hard workers.
12. They have always been great scholars.
13. The Germans have led the world in science.
14. Many great works of literature have been written by the Germans.
15. Some of the world's most beautiful music was composed by German composers.
16. The eastern part of Germany is the Communist part.
17. The largest city of Germany is Berlin which is divided into two sections.
18. Bonn is the capital of West Germany.
19. Cologne is famous for its old cathedral.
20. Germany would be a nice place to visit.

Declarative Sentences

A declarative sentence states a fact.

Circle the words that should be capitalized. Punctuate each sentence.

(our) body is truly incredible.

1. the human body is like a machine
2. its working parts can do useful work
3. your body needs food and oxygen
4. the human body is very complex
5. man could never build anything this complex
6. the body is made up of flesh, blood and bones
7. the bones form the skeleton
8. the skeleton is the framework on which the body is built
9. your skeleton is joined together to keep the body firm
10. the human body is about three-quarters water
11. some important substances are calcium, phosphorus and carbon
12. food that you eat must be organic matter
13. some parts of the food are stored in the body
14. our lungs take in oxygen
15. the heart is a mighty pump
16. the body is protected by an outside covering called skin
17. man is capable of reasoning because of his brain
18. humans have the ability to reproduce
19. our bodies can overcome diseases
20. we must take care of all our parts

10

Imperative Sentences

An imperative sentence is one that gives a command.
Put the dishes on the table.

Pick out the imperative sentences from the following list. Write the name **imperative** on the line in front of those sentences. Do not mark in the spaces before the other types of sentences.

_____ 1. Would you like to go on a camping trip?

_____ 2. Living close to nature can be fun.

_____ 3. Plan such trips carefully.

_____ 4. Choose a campsite suitable to your interests.

_____ 5. Some people like to fish or hunt.

_____ 6. Others like to swim or hike.

_____ 7. Have you ever gone canoeing on a camping trip?

_____ 8. It is important to bring the necessary equipment for a camping trip.

_____ 9. Pack the supplies with care.

_____ 10. Bring comfortable and durable clothes.

_____ 11. Blankets and sleeping bags are necessary.

_____ 12. Pack foods that are not easily spoiled.

_____ 13. Don't forget the pots, pans, dishes and utensils.

_____ 14. Never leave behind your compass and first aid kit.

_____ 15. Look for a safe and convenient area for the tent.

_____ 16. Set up the tent properly.

_____ 17. It will be your home on the trip.

_____ 18. Did you follow the directions carefully?

_____ 19. Check to make sure the campfire is out before leaving the campsite.

_____ 20. Many forest fires have been caused by careless campers.

Interrogative Sentences

Name _____

An interrogative sentence asks a question.

Circle the words that should be capitalized. Add correct ending punctuation.

(have) you ever visited (michigan) the (wolverine) (state)

1. did you know missouri is the show-me state
2. what state is the land of opportunity
3. where is the volunteer state
4. why do they call indiana the hoosier state
5. did you know that louisiana is the bayou state
6. what state is the sunshine state
7. where is the constitution state located
8. why would a state be called the dairy state
9. did you know utah is the beehive state
10. where is the lone star state
11. is south carolina the palmetto state
12. where do you think little rhody got its name
13. would you like to live in the golden state
14. where is the prairie state
15. would you be rich if you lived in the gem state
16. is the aloha state a nice place to visit
17. why is the sunflower state so flat
18. did you ever sing the iowa corn song
19. where would you find the empire state
20. did you know maine is the pine tree state

Exclamatory Sentences

Name _____

> An exclamatory sentence is one that expresses strong emotion.
>   Sometimes interrogative and exclamatory sentences begin with similar words.

Identify the sentences. Write **exclamatory, interrogative** or **imperative** on the lines. Place the correct punctuation mark after each sentence.

What a wonderful surprise!

_____ 1. Have you ever been in a cavern

_____ 2. How large the cave is

_____ 3. What forms such big caves

_____ 4. How are large caverns formed

_____ 5. What an amazing feat of nature

_____ 6. How far are we below the surface of the ground

_____ 7. How are different rooms formed within a cave

_____ 8. Be careful as you walk through the cavern

_____ 9. Don't get separated from the rest of the group

_____ 10. What thick walls divide the rooms of the cave

_____ 11. What beautiful icicles hang from the roof of the cavern

_____ 12. How were these stone icicles named stalactites

_____ 13. What are the names of the stone icicles growing up from the floor of the cave

_____ 14. How many years does it take to form stalactites and stalagmites

_____ 15. How pretty are the colors of the stone icicles

_____ 16. What forms the flower-like crystals on the walls

_____ 17. How delicate these shapes appear

_____ 18. How interesting caves are

_____ 19. How I enjoyed my first trip through a cave

_____ 20. Come with me on my next trip

Types of Sentences

Name _____

A declarative sentence states a fact. It is followed by a period.
An interrogative sentence askes a question. It is followed by a question mark.
An imperative sentence gives a command. It is followed by a period.
An exclamatory sentence expresses sudden or strong emotion. It is followed by an exclamation point.

Label each type of sentence. Place the proper punctuation mark at the end.

_____ 1. There are twelve months in a year

_____ 2. Can you name the months in order

_____ 3. Write the names of the months on your paper

_____ 4. What beautiful handwriting this is

_____ 5. Our vacation time is during the summer months

_____ 6. Are you planning a trip for this summer

_____ 7. What a great time we had last year

_____ 8. Tell me about your experiences on the trip

_____ 9. We toured the western United States

_____ 10. Our first stop was the Grand Canyon

_____ 11. How high the canyon walls stand

_____ 12. Have you ever visited the Grand Canyon

_____ 13. We spent part of our vacation camping in Colorado

_____ 14. Do you like to camp

_____ 15. What a memorable time we had last summer

_____ 16. We spend nearly nine months of the year in school

_____ 17. This time is spent learning many new things

_____ 18. A good education will open new opportunities for us

_____ 19. Write a composition about this school year

_____ 20. How quickly the year seems to pass

Simple and Compound Sentences

A simple sentence contains one subject and one predicate.

Colleen collects foreign stamps.

A compound sentence contains two independent sentences which are closely related. A conjuction usually joins the two clauses of a compound sentence.

The wind blew hard, and the rain poured down.

Label each sentence below as a simple or a compound sentence. In the compound sentences, circle the conjunction which joins the clauses.

_____ 1. Many children fly kites for fun.

_____ 2. We don't know who invented the kite, but the Chinese used a flat kite 2000 years ago.

_____ 3. The Chinese enjoy flying kites very much, and they have a national holiday called Kites' Day.

_____ 4. Kites have meant a great deal to the people of China, Japan and Korea.

_____ 5. Even grown-ups fly kites in these countries.

_____ 6. Kites are used as toys, but they have been used for other purposes, too.

_____ 7. The ancient Chinese flew kites to drive away evil spirits.

_____ 8. Weather Bureaus have used kites to send weather instruments high into the air.

_____ 9. A kite played an important part in a very famous experiment.

_____ 10. Benjamin Franklin flew a kite during a thunderstorm, and he discovered that lightning was a spark of electricity.

_____ 11. Ordinary flat kites must have tails.

_____ 12. The tail weighs down the lower end, and this helps to keep the kite from nose-diving.

_____ 13. Box kites do not need tails.

_____ 14. Many kites are brightly decorated.

_____ 15. The Chinese sometimes attach streamers to their kites.

_____ 16. Wind is needed for kite flying.

_____ 17. A day with gentle breezes is best for kite flying.

_____ 18. It is fun to fly kites, and they are interesting to watch.

15

Use of Capital Letters and Periods

Name _____

Use a capital letter for the first word of every sentence, all proper nouns and proper adjectives. Capitilize initials and abbreviations when capitals would be used if the words were written in full.
Place a period after declarative and imperative sentences, abbreviations and initials.

Circle each letter which should be a capital and place periods where they are needed.

1. only one man has been the president of the u s for more than two terms
2. his parents were james and sara d roosevelt
3. his name was franklin d roosevelt
4. the family lived in new york
5. after graduating from harvard university, he attended columbia law school
6. he married a distant cousin, eleanor roosevelt
7. they had five children, anna, james, elliot, franklin and john
8. roosevelt was asked by president woodrow wilson to work in washington, d c
9. in 1928, roosevelt was elected governor of new york
10. four years later, he became the 32nd u s president
11. by the time roosevelt had finished his second term, world war II was underway
12. on dec 7, 1941 the japanese attacked pearl harbor
13. this attack brought the u s into the war
14. the american people were unwilling to change presidents during such a time
15. f d roosevelt was re-elected to a third term
16. he lead the united states of america through many months of the war
17. not surprisingly, f d r was chosen for a fourth term in office
18. however, he didn't live to see the end of world war II
19. he died on apr 12, 1945 in warm springs, georgia
20. franklin d roosevelt has been honored by americans and other people around the world

Recognizing Nouns

> A noun is a word which names a person, place or thing.
>   person: girl, policeman, neighbor
>   place: kitchen, city, zoo
>   thing: desk, pen, fence

The words below are nouns. Write each one in the proper column to show whether it names a person, place or thing.

	Person	Place	Thing
1. voters			
2. United States			
3. lawyer			
4. cabin			
5. America			
6. year			
7. Abraham Lincoln			
8. speech			
9. theater			
10. president			

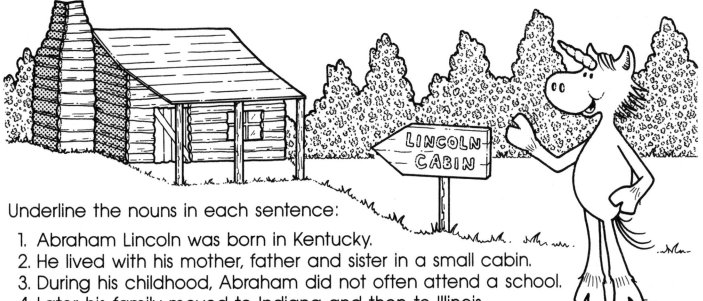

Underline the nouns in each sentence:

1. Abraham Lincoln was born in Kentucky.
2. He lived with his mother, father and sister in a small cabin.
3. During his childhood, Abraham did not often attend a school.
4. Later his family moved to Indiana and then to Illinois.
5. Abraham Lincoln worked as a clerk and then became a lawyer.
6. He was elected a congressman for the state of Illinois.
7. Abraham Lincoln became the President of the United States in the year 1861.
8. The Civil War was fought while Lincoln was president.
9. Lincoln gave his famous speech, the Gettysburg Address, in November of 1863.
10. In April, 1865, John Wilkes Booth shot the president as he watched a play at Ford's Theatre in Washington, D.C.

17

Proper and Common Nouns

Name _____

A proper noun names a particular person, place or thing.
A common noun names any one of a class of persons, places or things.

Columbus Finds America

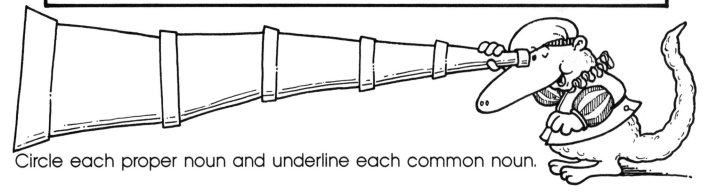

Circle each proper noun and underline each common noun.

1. Christopher Columbus came to Lisbon, Portugal, because he was interested in the sea and ships.
2. He enjoyed stories the sailors told about their adventures to Asia and Africa.
3. Columbus read a book about the adventures of Marco Polo in China and India.
4. Columbus believed the world was round while the others disbelieved.
5. King Ferdinand and Queen Isabella granted Columbus permission to explore new routes to the Far East.
6. They sailed on three ships: the Santa Maria, Pinta and the Nina.
7. The caravels left on a misty morning in August, 1492.
8. The sailors knew the Atlantic Ocean from Spain to the Canary Islands.
9. Columbus landed in America on October 12, 1492.
10. He thought for sure he was in Japan.
11. Columbus did not understand why there were no gold roofs on houses as in the book by Marco Polo.
12. When Columbus returned to Barcelona, the sound of trumpets and drums greeted him.
13. The king and queen were pleased with his discovery.
14. His fame spread over Europe.
15. Columbus made three more voyages to the West.
16. He found more islands and explored the shores of South America and Central America.
17. Columbus died after his fourth voyage.
18. He died without knowing that he discovered one of the richest continents of the world.
19. We honor Christopher Columbus as the discoverer of the New World.
20. Many cities, towns and buildings have been named in his honor.

Abstract and Concrete Nouns

> Nouns can also be classified as concrete or abstract.
> A concrete noun names something that can be seen or touched.
> An abstract noun names a condition, quality or action separate
>   from any other object.
>
> | <u>Concrete Nouns</u> | <u>Abstract Nouns</u> |
> |---|---|
> | tree, picture, animal | courtesy, knowledge, beauty |

Write the word abstract or concrete in order to label it correctly.

appreciation	_____	truth	_____
Mexico	_____	pilot	_____
freedom	_____	museum	_____
happiness	_____	intelligence	_____
flowers	_____	photograph	_____
enthusiasm	_____	garden	_____
doctor	_____	honesty	_____

In the following sentences, circle the concrete nouns and underline the abstract nouns.

1. Once during the childhood of Benjamin Franklin, he met another boy blowing a whistle.
2. Franklin offered the child all the pennies in his pocket for the toy.
3. The boy agreed, and Ben felt much pride with this accomplishment.
4. Later, he felt much unhappiness upon learning he had paid enough to buy four whistles at the store.
5. Ben Franklin was not a person to show discouragement.
6. He came to show great wisdom.
7. Benjamin Franklin gave much time to winning freedom and glory for his native land.
8. He invented stoves, discovered lightning was electricity, and made lightning rods.
9. He founded the first public library, the first fire department and the first magazine.
10. No man ever did so much for the comfort and benefit of others.

Persons of Nouns

Name _____

> Person is the quality of a noun through which the speaker, the one spoken to, or the one spoken about is indicated.
> 1. The first person refers to the speaker.
> 2. The second person refers to the one spoken to.
> 3. The third person refers to the one spoken about.

On the line before each sentence, write the person of the underlined noun.

_____ 1. The <u>Declaration of Independence</u> was signed on July 14, 1776.

_____ 2. We, <u>Americans</u>, were given many freedoms through this document.

_____ 3. <u>Students</u>, have you seen the document at the Smithsonian Institute?

_____ 4. Yes, our <u>class</u> visited this museum last May.

_____ 5. In 1775, the <u>Contintental Congress</u> was formed.

_____ 6. The <u>representatives</u> met the following year to continue their efforts towards independence.

_____ 7. We, <u>colonists</u>, wanted complete freedom from England.

_____ 8. The Declaration of Independence told why the <u>colonies</u> wanted to be free.

_____ 9. <u>Class</u>, do you know the reasons why we wanted our freedom?

_____10. <u>Pupils</u>, do you know the wrongs that were suffered by the colonists?

_____ 11. The Declaration of Independence stated the <u>colonies</u> would become an independent nation.

_____ 12. <u>Thomas Jefferson</u> did most of the writing with the help of John Adams and Benjamin Franklin.

_____ 13. We, <u>citizens</u>, are indebted to these men and those who signed.

_____ 14. Fifty-six <u>men</u> signed the Declaration.

_____ 15. We, <u>countrymen</u>, have greatly benefited from the Declaration of Independence.

Persons of Nouns

> Person is the quality of a noun through which the speaker, the one spoken to, or the one spoken about is indicated.
> The first person refers to the speaker.
> The second person refers to the one spoken to.
> The third person refers to the one (person, place or thing) spoken about.

On the line before each sentence, write the person of the underlined noun.

____ 1. One way of telling a <u>story</u> is to present it as a stage performance.

____ 2. Such a performance is called a <u>play</u>.

____ 3. <u>Children</u>, have you ever seen a play?

____ 4. Plays are usually given in a <u>theater</u>.

____ 5. We, the <u>audience</u>, must watch and listen carefully.

____ 6. The first theaters were built by the ancient <u>Greeks</u>.

____ 7. During the Middle Ages, the <u>people</u> of Europe became interested in acting.

____ 8. Many of the plays at this time told <u>stories</u> from the Bible.

____ 9. During the time of <u>William Shakespeare</u> no women acted in plays.

____ 10. <u>Boys</u>, have you ever thought of performing on stage?

____ 11. We, <u>girls</u>, now have the opportunity to become actresses.

____ 12. Today, much acting is done before a <u>camera</u> instead of an audience.

____ 13. Many actors appear on <u>television</u>.

____ 14. A really great <u>actor</u> makes us forget who he is while performing.

____ 15. We, the <u>listeners</u>, concentrate only on the part he is playing.

____ 16. The actor allows us to understand the <u>character</u> in the play.

____ 17. We can also understand the <u>emotions</u> felt by the character.

____ 18. Acting is now thought of as an <u>art</u>.

____ 19. We, <u>Americans</u>, pay great actors as much honor as we pay great painters or musicians.

____ 20. <u>Ladies</u> and <u>gentlemen</u>, let's have a round of applause for this play.

____ 21. The theater and acting are always a thrill for us <u>spectators</u>.

Number

> Number is the quality of a noun which indicates whether it refers to one person, place or thing, or more than one.
> A singular noun denotes one person, place or thing.
> A plural noun denotes more than one person, place or thing.
>
> | Singular Nouns | | Plural Nouns | |
> |---|---|---|---|
> | bat | box | bats | boxes |
> | picture | gas | pictures | gases |
> | apple | peach | apples | peaches |

Write **S** for singular and **P** for plural of the following nouns.

dishes	patches
porch	radio
house	sons
pencils	teacher
axes	soldier
knives	cup

Underline the following nouns. Place **S** above the singular nouns and **P** above the plural nouns.

1. California has a coastline stretching along the Pacific Ocean for more than 1,000 miles.

2. The Spanish first settled this area, followed by the Mexicans.

3. California became the 31st state in 1850.

4. Pioneers headed for California in the 1840's to look for gold.

5. Newcomers found the region very pleasant.

6. California farmers and fishermen lead the states in the dollar value of their products.

7. The most valuable crop in California is cotton; followed by citrus fruits.

8. The lowest land in the United States is found in California. It is known as Death Valley.

9. There are four national parks in California.

10. This state is an interesting place for people to visit.

Number of Nouns

Name _____

Number is the quality of a noun which indicates whether it refers to one person, place or thing, or more than one.

Singular nouns refer to one and plural nouns refer to more than one.

Singular Nouns		Plural Nouns	
suggestion	hero	suggestions	heroes
wish	sheep	wishes	sheep
half	man	halves	men
colony		colonies	

Write each of the following words in the proper column and form the matching singular or plural noun.

Singular	Plural		Singular	Plural
1. trick		8. child		
2. life		9. shelves		
3. echo		10. cities		
4. curtains		11. attorney		
5. classes		12. porch		
6. deer		13. feet		
7. duty		14. countries		

Underline the nouns in the following sentences and label each as singular or plural. Place an **S** above the singular nouns and a **P** above the plural nouns.

1. There are mountains that shoot out streams of hot rock and ashes.
2. These mountains are called volcanoes.
3. People of long ago made up stories to explain them.
4. Each volcano forms in much the same way.
5. Gases deep in the earth force molten rock through an opening in the ground.
6. The red-hot rock that pours from volcanoes is called lava.
7. When lava cools into solid rock, it forms piles around the opening.
8. In time, the piles become a cone-shaped mountain.
9. At the top of the volcanic cone is a hollow called a crater.
10. Volcanoes can build themselves on land or rise from the bottom of oceans and seas.

Gender of Nouns

> Gender is the quality of a noun through which sex is indicated. There are three genders: masculine which denotes the male sex, feminine which denotes the female sex and neuter which denotes objects which have no sex.
>
> A noun that may be either masculine or feminine is usually considered masculine unless otherwise noted in the context of a sentence.
>
> | Masculine Gender | Feminine Gender | Neuter Gender |
> |---|---|---|
> | husband | wife | home |
> | waiter | waitress | table |

Label each noun according to the correct gender.

1. grandfather
2. heroine
3. queen
4. carpet
5. nephew
6. statue
7. actress
8. emperor
9. newspaper
10. aunt
11. heir
12. princess
13. umbrella
14. sister
15. stallion
16. encyclopedia

Underline the nouns in the following sentences and label each according to its gender. Place an **M** above the nouns denoting masculine gender, **F** above the nouns denoting feminine gender, and **N** above the nouns denoting neuter gender.

1. Dolly Payne was a little girl who lived in Virginia during the Revolutionary War.
2. When she grew up, she married James Madison.
3. He became the fourth President of the United States.
4. They lived in the new city built on the banks of the Potomac River.
5. This city was named after George Washington.
6. The president and his wife shared a new home called the White House.
7. A valuable painting of George Washington hung in the dining room.
8. During the War of 1812, English soldiers marched through the streets of the city.
9. Before they reached the capital, Dolly placed the famous picture in her carriage.
10. This brave lady left behind her own belongings.
11. Dolly Madison became one of the best-loved women in American history.

Nouns Used as Subjects
and Predicate Nominatives

> Case is the quality of a noun that shows its relationship to some other word in the sentence. There are three cases: nominative case, possessive case and objective case.
>
> A noun used as the subject of a verb is in the nominative case.

Draw a line under the nouns used as subjects in the following sentences.

A sudden <u>storm</u> appeared on the horizon.

1. Many stories have been written about Paul Bunyan.
2. Once, a blue snow fell in his North Woods.
3. The forest animals fled farther north.
4. Some bears became polar bears.
5. Paul discovered a blue calf during the storm.
6. The big man cared for the calf named Babe.
7. Soon the calf grew very large.
8. Babe became Paul's constant companion.
9. News about Paul and Babe traveled far.
10. Paul Bunyan was known as the greatest logger of all time.

> A noun used as a predicate nominative is in the nominative case. The noun that follows a linking verb and refers to the same person or thing as the subject is the predicate nominative.

In the following sentences, underline the subject and circle the predicate nominative.

The <u>winner</u> of the contest is (Mary.)

1. "Gulliver's Travels" is a famous story.
2. The author is Jonathan Swift.
3. The book is a story of adventure.
4. A long sea voyage was the setting.
5. The land of Lilliput was not the planned destination.
6. The main character was Gulliver.
7. This voyager was now a prisoner in Lilliput.
8. Later, the man was the friend of the emperor.
9. Many Lilliputians were helpers in preparing for Gulliver's departure.
10. The seafarer was an Englishman returned home at last.

25

Direct Address

> A noun used in direct address is in the nominative case.
> Sharon, please close the door.

Underline the noun in direct address.
    Where are the keys, <u>John</u>?

1. Erika, when was New Orleans founded?
2. The city was begun in 1718, Megan.
3. For forty years, Anthony, the city was controlled by the French.
4. Then the French turned it over to the Spanish, Jones.
5. Sammy, the Spanish held the city for thirty years and then gave it back to the French.
6. The French, Charles, then sold it to the United States as part of the Louisiana Purchase.
7. New Orleans is on delta land built by the Mississippi River, Robert.
8. Mary, New Orleans was an important port from its beginning.
9. Ocean vessels, Jason, could sail up the river to it.
10. Riverboats can reach it easily, Lori.
11. Mark, the very first steamboat on the Mississippi was named the "New Orleans".
12. Today, Kyle, New Orleans is a city of more than half a million people.
13. Rebecca, it is still a leading southern port of the United States.
14. Tourists visit New Orleans, Shawna, by the thousands.
15. Each year, during the week before Lent, Melissa, the city has a carnival.
16. This carnival is called the Mardi Gras, Nicholas.
17. It is the gayest festival in all the United States, Sue.
18. Jane, one part of the celebration is a grand parade down Canal Street.
19. At Mardi Gras time, Latriece, visitors crowd into the city.
20. Christie, these visitors help make New Orleans a prosperous city.

26

Appositives in the Nominative Case

Name _____

> A noun in apposition is in the same case as the noun it explains.
> A noun in apposition with the subject or predicate nominative is in the nominative case.

Underline the appositive and circle the word it explains.

Tom (Dooley,) a <u>doctor</u>, treated the sick.
This is my (cousin,) <u>Donald</u>

1. One man, Leonardo DaVinci, represents civilization during the Renaissance.
2. DaVinci, the painter, was also the first engineer of his time.
3. Andrea del Verrocchio, a famous artist, was Leonardo's tutor.
4. DaVinci's patron was Lodovico Sforza, the Duke of Milan.
5. A patron, the artist's employer, assigned the projects to be completed.
6. The projects, oil paintings, were requested by the Duke.
7. Leonardo, the observer, kept many books of notes and drawings.
8. These notes, scientific observations, were not translated into English until the late 1800's.
9. DaVinci, a genius, was not truly appreciated for hundred of years.
10. Leonardo was also an astronomer, a gazer of stars.
11. Leonardo, the architect, designed an elaborate revolving stage.
12. This great man was also an aeronautical engineer, a designer of flying machines.
13. The spring-driven helix, the first helicoptor, was his invention.
14. A military engineer, DaVinci, designed advanced war machines.
15. One such machine, an armored tank, was well ahead of the times.
16. Botany, the study of plants, also interested Leonardo DaVinci.
17. It is DaVinci, the artist, that is most admired.
18. A painting, the "Mona Lisa", is surrounded by legends.
19. The "Last Supper", a masterpiece, is best known.
20. This mural, his greatest creation, was badly damaged.

Use of Comma with Words
in Direct Address and Apposition

> A comma is used to set off words in direct address.
> Clean your room, Jill.
> Jill, put your things in order.
> Clean your room, Jill, and put your things in order.

Insert commas to show the words in direct address.

1. Today students we will discuss inventors.
2. Joan do you know who invented the telephone?
3. Alexander Graham Bell was the inventor Rose.
4. No one is really sure who invented the printing press Nichole.
5. Some people believe class that it was invented by Johann Geutenberg.
6. Kari another important inventor was Thomas Edison.
7. Were you aware Jimmy that he invented the phonograph?
8. Robert the television does not have a single inventor.
9. Three people are credited with its development Melissa.
10. Their names boys and girls are Vladimir Zworykin, John L. Bair and Philo J. Farnsworth.

> Commas are used to set off words in apposition.
> The Louvre, a large museum, is in France.

1. Two brothers Orville and Wilbur Wright invented the airplane.
2. Eli Whitney the inventor of the cotton gin attended Yale University.
3. The radio was invented by Marconi an Italian.
4. Robert Fulton the inventor of the steamboat was an American.
5. Thomas Edison the inventor of the light bulb also developed the movie projector.
6. Walter Hunt invented a tiny device the safety pin.
7. A Frenchman Francois Blanchard invented the parachute.
8. Samuel Morse an American is responsible for the telegraph.
9. An important weather gauge the barometer was invented in 1643.
10. W.H. Carothers developed nylon a lightweight material.

Direct Object

> A noun can be used as the object word in a sentence. The word which answers the question "whom" or "what" after the verb is the Direct Object.

Circle the Direct Object in each sentence.

1. People like frozen desserts.
2. Marco Polo brought recipes home from the Far East.
3. Many ices contain fruit juices.
4. Dolly Madison served ice cream at a party in the 1800's.
5. Americans choose ice cream as their favorite dessert.
6. Americans eat three billion quarts a year.
7. People make ice cream from milk and cream.
8. Sugar, fruit and nuts give flavor to ice cream.
9. Egg and gelatin make the ice cream smooth.
10. People may choose different flavors of ice cream.
11. Most people choose vanilla.
12. One big chain of restaurants advertises 40 different flavors of ice cream.
13. Today, large ice cream plants produce this product.
14. Big milk trucks bring the milk and cream to the plants.
15. Other trucks bring the different ingredients to be used in the ice cream.
16. Often people eat ice cream as a dessert for meals.
17. People make ice cream into milkshakes.
18. Some ingredients make fancy desserts like parfaits.
19. We would miss this treat if we didn't have it.
20. Do you like ice cream?

Nouns Used as Direct Objects

A noun which acts as the direct object of a verb is in the objective case. The word which answers the question "whom" or "what" after the verb is the direct object.

Underline the verb and circle the direct object in each sentence below.
The boy <u>put</u> the (skates) on the shelf.

1. The people of the United States own the White House.
2. Many tourists visit this home each year.
3. James Hoban designed the plans.
4. Gray sandstone forms the walls.
5. The building was called the President's Palace.
6. The wife of President Adams hung her washing in a room that later became the East Room.
7. Fire damaged the structure during the War of 1812.
8. White paint hid the stains from the smoke.
9. Later presidents added more rooms to the White House.
10. President Harry Truman ordered repairs for the house.
11. A steel framework now supports the walls.
12. Steel also strengthens the roof.
13. The whole interior needed improvements.
14. Workers built offices for the president and his helpers.
15. The president uses the building as a home and a workplace.
16. The president greets guests in the Blue Room.
17. Blue silk covers the walls in the Blue Room.
18. The State Dining Room holds many people.
19. Americans admire the beauty of the White House.
20. Visitors respect this symbol of our nation.

30

Possessive Nouns

> A noun that expresses possession or ownership is in the possessive case.
>   To form the singular possessive, add 's to the singular noun.
>   To form the plural possessive of nouns ending in s, add only an apostrophe. If the plural does not end in s, add 's.

Write the singular possessive, the plural and the plural possessive forms of the following nouns.

Singular	Singular Possessive	Plural	Plural Possessive
boy	boy's	boys	boys'

1. student
2. child
3. neighbor
4. baby
5. writer
6. uncle
7. mouse
8. lady
9. man
10. leaf

Underline the nouns in the possessive case.
        Marina's book is on the desk.

1. Henry Wadsworth Longfellow is one of America's famous writers.
2. Longfellow's poems have been enjoyed by many people.
3. His two sons and three daughters are mentioned in "The Children's Hour".
4. Another of Longfellow's poems is "Paul Revere's Ride".
5. "Evangeline" is the story of one woman's courage.

Rewrite each phrase so that there is a noun in the possessive case.
        the song of the bird   the bird's song

1. the mane of the lion
2. the votes of the citizens
3. the words of the speaker
4. the home of my grandparents
5. the dresses of the women

Possessives

> A noun that expresses possession or ownership is in the possessive case.
>   To form the singular possessive, add 's to the nominative singular of the noun.
>   To form the plural possessive of nouns ending in s, add only an apostrophe. If the nominative plural does not end in s, add 's.

Write the singular possessive, the plural and the plural possessive forms.

Singular	Singular Possessive	Plural	Plural Possessive
1. teacher			
2. baby			
3. child			
4. woman			
5. team			
6. friend			
7. man			
8. dog			
9. girl			
10. doctor			

Underline the possessive form of the noun in each sentence.

1. Booker T. Washington is one of America's famous black men.
2. Washington's book <u>Up From Slavery</u> tells the story of his life.
3. He became the slaves' spokesman.
4. Washington traveled around the world telling of the Negroes' problems.
5. Washington's formal education was at Hampton Institute for Negroes.
6. Booker's grades were very high.
7. He became one of the school's leading teachers.
8. He founded a Negroes' school in 1881 in Tuskegee, Alabama.
9. The first classes were held in a church's meeting room.
10 The school's name became Tuskegee Institute.

Nouns Used as Objects of Prepositions

A noun used as the object of a preposition is in the objective case. The word that answers the question "whom" or "what" after the preposition is the object of that preposition.

In the following sentences, underline the preposition and circle its object.
The jet roared <u>across</u> the (sky.)

1. Weather is often a topic for discussion.
2. Rain and snow are a part of the weather.
3. Clouds, heat waves and periods of cold also affect the weather.
4. People must prepare for quick changes in the weather.
5. Not everyone wants the same kind of weather.
6. A farmer may hope for rain.
7. His neighbor might want sunny weather for a picnic.
8. Some people may wish for a heavy snowstorm for skiing.
9. Not everyone likes warm weather in early spring.
10. They know snow in the mountains may melt too quickly.
11. This could result in floods.
12. Weather is an important factor in a person's life.
13. Bad weather may ruin crops and raise the cost of food.
14. It may cause forest fires or kill livestock on the ranges.
15. The weather affects our lives in many ways.
16. In the summer, people complain about the humidity.
17. Humidity is the amount of moisture in the air.
18. A warm day seems hotter with higher humidity.
19. Inside our homes, we can control certain factors.
20. We have learned much from scientific experiments.

33

Nouns Used as Indirect Objects

> A noun which acts as an indirect object is in the objective case. The indirect object indicates to whom or for whom the action is performed.

Underline the direct object and circle the indirect object.
The teacher gave (Susan) the <u>book</u>.

1. Thomas Edison gave the world many useful inventions.
2. He gave man a better means of lighting.
3. Candles gave people light in earlier times.
4. Kerosene gave lamps the necessary fuel to burn.
5. Edison paid his assistants money to research better lighting.
6. These helpers offered Edison information they found.
7. Edison gave people the electric light bulb.
8. Edison offered mankind many other ideas to save time and energy.
9. His experiments provided men an easier way of life.
10. We owe Thomas Edison our gratitude.

Appositive in the Objective Case

> A noun in apposition with a direct object, indirect object or object of a preposition is in the objective case.

Circle the noun in apposition and <u>underline</u> the word it explains.
We need the <u>device</u>, the (telephone.)

1. An important device was discovered by the famous inventor, Alexander Graham Bell.
2. Alexander G. Bell invented a modern-day tool, the telephone.
3. Bell was born in a foreign country, Scotland.
4. At night, he worked on his favorite hobby, electricity.
5. Bell had an assistant, Thomas Watson.
6. Watson built an instrument, the harmonic telegraph, for Bell.
7. Together, they worked on this project, the telephone.
8. Watson heard sounds, the first words, over the telephone.
9. Years later, Bell talked to Watson across lines in another city, San Francisco.
10. Alexander Graham Bell will be remembered as a great man, the inventor of the telephone.

Recognition of Verbs

Name _____

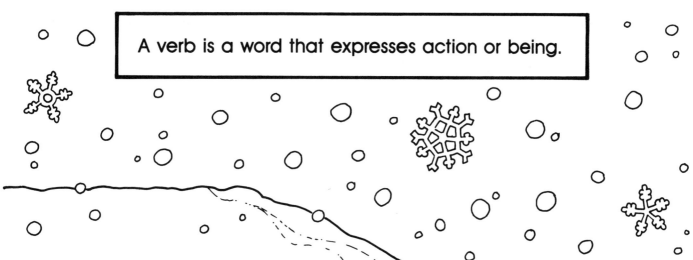

A verb is a word that expresses action or being.

Circle the verb in each sentence. Tell if it is an action **A** verb or a being **B** verb.

____ 1. Many people play summer sports.

____ 2. However, there are many winter sports.

____ 3. Skiing and skating are popular.

____ 4. Skating is an old sport.

____ 5. Some skaters work for faster speeds.

____ 6. Other skaters like figure skating better.

____ 7. Figure skating is fancy skating.

____ 8. Many people enjoy ice hockey.

____ 9. Skating is an important part of this sport.

____ 10. Players shoot a puck into a goal net.

____ 11. Boys and girls coast down snowy hills on sleds.

____ 12. Toboggans are fun, too.

____ 13. Skiing is another favorite winter sport.

____ 14. Skiing down slopes takes great skill.

____ 15. Ski jumpers leap high into the air.

____ 16. They sail gracefully through the air.

____ 17. The landing is tricky.

____ 18. Contestants participate in the Winter Olympics.

____ 19. These games happen every four years.

____ 20. People watch the Olympics with much interest.

Action and Being Verbs

> A verb is a word which expresses action or being. The verb is the most important word in a sentence. There can be no sentence without the verb.

Write **S** on the line before each group of words which is a sentence and underline the verb in each. Write **N** on the line before each group of words that is not a sentence.

<u>N</u> Across the bridge   <u>S</u> We walked across the bridge.

____ 1. Paul Revere was a patriotic American

____ 2. The ride of Paul Revere

____ 3. Revere lived in Boston during the time of the American Revolution

____ 4. He belonged to a group of patriots

____ 5. Part of the Boston Tea Party

____ 6. The British troops in Boston

____ 7. The tea party was a warning to England

____ 8. The colonists wanted some say in their own government

____ 9. Orders of the English king

____10. The colonists fought for their freedom

Underline the verb in each sentence and tell whether it is an action verb or a being verb.

<u>action</u> The wolf <u>howled</u> in the distance.   <u>being</u> A wolf <u>is</u> an animal.

____ 1. The colonists stored ammunition at Concord, near Boston.

____ 2. The minutemen were American soldiers ready for battle.

____ 3. The British army was on the march.

____ 4. They wanted the ammunition at Concord.

____ 5. Paul Revere was the messenger of the patriots.

____ 6. He watched for the signal from Old North Church in Boston.

____ 7. Two lanterns flashed in the church tower.

____ 8. He raced to the minutemen.

____ 9. The British came by water.

____10. Paul Revere warned the American soldiers in time.

Review of Verbs

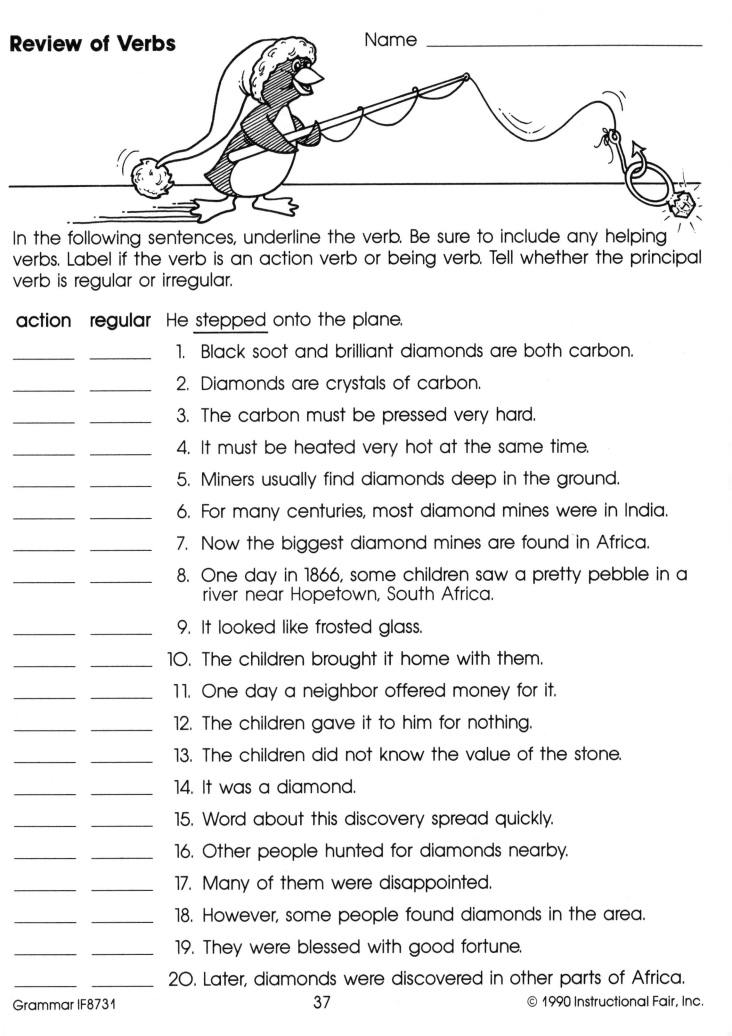

Name _____

In the following sentences, underline the verb. Be sure to include any helping verbs. Label if the verb is an action verb or being verb. Tell whether the principal verb is regular or irregular.

action **regular** He <u>stepped</u> onto the plane.

_____ _____ 1. Black soot and brilliant diamonds are both carbon.

_____ _____ 2. Diamonds are crystals of carbon.

_____ _____ 3. The carbon must be pressed very hard.

_____ _____ 4. It must be heated very hot at the same time.

_____ _____ 5. Miners usually find diamonds deep in the ground.

_____ _____ 6. For many centuries, most diamond mines were in India.

_____ _____ 7. Now the biggest diamond mines are found in Africa.

_____ _____ 8. One day in 1866, some children saw a pretty pebble in a river near Hopetown, South Africa.

_____ _____ 9. It looked like frosted glass.

_____ _____ 10. The children brought it home with them.

_____ _____ 11. One day a neighbor offered money for it.

_____ _____ 12. The children gave it to him for nothing.

_____ _____ 13. The children did not know the value of the stone.

_____ _____ 14. It was a diamond.

_____ _____ 15. Word about this discovery spread quickly.

_____ _____ 16. Other people hunted for diamonds nearby.

_____ _____ 17. Many of them were disappointed.

_____ _____ 18. However, some people found diamonds in the area.

_____ _____ 19. They were blessed with good fortune.

_____ _____ 20. Later, diamonds were discovered in other parts of Africa.

Verb Phrases

> A group of words that do the job of a single verb is called a verb phrase. In a verb phrase, there is one principal verb and one or more helping verbs.

Circle the verb phrase in each sentence.

These sentences (were written) about Rudyard Kipling.

1. Rudyard Kipling was born in Bombay, India.
2. His English father was teaching art in India.
3. Kipling had heard jungle stories from the native people.
4. The Indian people had told these stories to their own children.
5. At the age of six, Rudyard was sent to school in England.
6. However, he could not attend school.
7. He had become very ill.
8. Kipling could not go to school for 5 years.
9. After many years, he had completed his basic education.
10. At this time, Kipling's father was working in Lahore, India.
11. Rudyard would return to that country.
12. His job in India would be writing for a newspaper.
13. He had written several poems and short stories for the newspaper.
14. Later, these poems and stories were published in two books.
15. He had become famous by the age of 26.
16. One of his most famous books was written for his children.
17. That book is called The Jungle Book.
18. Captains Courageous was written during his years in Vermont.
19. After a few years in America, Kipling had planned a return to England.
20. Rudyard Kipling is loved around the world for his children's stories.

38

Verb Phrases

A group of words that does the job of a single verb is called a verb phrase. In a verb phrase, there is one principal verb and one or more helping or auxiliary verbs.

Circle the verb phrases in the following sentences.

The tourists (had lost) their way.

1. Laws are made for the good of the people.
2. Without rules, there would be many arguments.
3. This need has resulted in new laws.
4. Laws have made an impact on our daily lives.
5. In ancient times, a ruler could make a new law by his own decision.
6. Today, people can share in the decision about a new law.
7. However, not everyone can agree about the law.
8. People in our country may vote on their opinion.
9. A law can be passed even without everyone's consent.
10. Almost every law has been broken at some time.
11. Therefore, courts must decide on appropriate penalties.
12. A person in the United States is living under three sets of laws.
13. City laws are called ordinances.
14. State laws are passed by the state legislature.
15. In addition, federal laws have been instituted.
16. No law can be enforced outside the Constitution.
17. Laws may become out of date.
18. Such laws could be repealed.
19. This can be accomplished by a vote of the people.
20. Throughout history, laws have been proven necessary for good order.

Regular Verbs

Name _____

> The principal parts of a verb are the present, past and past participle. A regular verb forms its past and past participle by adding **-d** or **-ed** to the present. The past participle always uses a helping verb with the main verb.

Write the past and past participle forms of the following verbs.

Present	Past	Past Participle (Always used with a helping verb)
bake	baked	baked

1. finish
2. call
3. open
4. delay
5. follow
6. gather
7. talk
8. stumble
9. help
10. whisper

Label the forms of the verbs.

like **present**
peeked **past**
had scrambled **past participle**

1. explored
2. wait
3. skated
4. have hurried
5. pick
6. had leaped
7. raced
8. has trimmed
9. sprinkle
10. had invented

Regular Verbs

Name _____

The principal parts of a verb are the present, past and past participle. A regular verb is one that forms its past and past participle by adding **-d** or **-ed** to the present. The past participle always uses a helping or auxiliary verb with the main verb.

Write the past and past participle forms of the following verbs.

Present	Past	Past Participle (used with auxiliary)
plan	planned	planned
hope	hoped	hoped

1. reach
2. climb
3. offer
4. cooperate
5. believe
6. walk
7. notice
8. move
9. appear
10. float
11. study
12. paint
13. clean
14. visit
15. call

Label the forms of the verbs below.

> stop — *present*
> placed — *past*
> has played — *past participle*

1. arranged
2. has delivered
3. watch
4. had assigned
5. pour
6. danced
7. scramble
8. have purchased
9. changed
10. suggest
11. covered
12. has listened
13. plunge
14. tested

Irregular Verbs

An irregular verb is one that does not form its past and past participle by adding -d or -ed to its present. The past participle form always uses a helping or auxiliary verb.

Write the past and past participle forms of these irregular verbs.

Present	Past	Past Participle (used with auxiliary)
do	did	done
see	_____	_____
go	_____	_____
bring	_____	_____
fall	_____	_____
run	_____	_____
make	_____	_____
forget	_____	_____
give	_____	_____
have	_____	_____
write	_____	_____
meet	_____	_____
know	_____	_____
speak	_____	_____
win	_____	_____
stand	_____	_____
take	_____	_____
sit	_____	_____
grow	_____	_____
choose	_____	_____
burst	_____	_____
freeze	_____	_____

Drill on Irregular Verbs

Name _____

The following sentences have irregular verbs. Underline the verb in each sentence. Label the principal verb according to its present, past or past participle form.

past
participle   Lighthouses <u>have sent</u> signals to ships.

_____ 1. Far out at sea, ships run into few dangers.

_____ 2. A bad storm makes a trip rough.

_____ 3. Many stories about sailing tell of shipwrecks on rocky coasts.

_____ 4. Many ships have sunk near dangerous reefs.

_____ 5. For hundreds of years, men have built lighthouses.

_____ 6. Lighthouses often have kept ships out of danger.

_____ 7. Their lights have shown faithfully through the years.

_____ 8. The earliest lighthouses had bonfires for light.

_____ 9. In time, candles took the place of bonfires.

_____ 10. Later, oil lamps came into use.

_____ 11. Then, electric lamps brought a convenient means of light.

_____ 12. Today, most lighthouses have electric lamps with lenses and reflectors.

_____ 13. Rocky islands have become the usual location for lighthouses.

_____ 14. Lighthouse keepers often led lonely lives.

_____ 15. Now most lights in lighthouses run automatically.

_____ 16. This gives the lighthouse keepers more free time.

_____ 17. However, bad weather still gives lighthouse keepers much work.

_____ 18. They send out radio signals to the ships.

_____ 19. The sound of the foghorn has kept many ships out of danger.

_____ 20. All around the world, sailors know the importance of lighthouses and their keepers.

Drill on Irregular Verbs

Name _____

In each of the following sentences, fill in the form of the irregular verb that is indicated.

I <u>saw</u> the parade.

1. George Washington _____ the location for the capital of the United States. (Past of choose)

2. He had _____ a site on the Potomac River. (Past participle of choose)

3. People have _____ the letters "D.C." after the name of this city. (Past participle of write)

4. The letters _____ for the "District of Columbia". (Present of stand)

5. The new government had _____ land from Virginia and Maryland as the site of the city. (Past participle of take)

6. Officials had _____ the job of city planner to Major L'Enfant. (Past participle of give)

7. Major L'Enfant had _____ out an interesting pattern for the streets. (Past participle of lay)

8. Many of them _____ out like spokes on a wheel. (Present of go)

9. Fine parks and buildings _____ the city extremely beautiful. (Present of make)

10. The government has _____ many of the buildings. (Past participle of build)

11. Washington _____ the official capital of the United States in 1800. (Past of become)

12. During the War of 1812, the city _____ into the hands of the British. (Past of fall)

13. The work of the national government has _____ . (Past participle of grow)

14. New buildings have been _____ from time to time. (Past participle of build)

15. Monuments _____ above other buildings. (Present of rise)

16. Pennsylvania Avenue has _____ the most famous street in Washington, D.C. (Past participle of become)

17. Many great parades have _____ down this avenue. (Past participle of go)

18. People have _____ for hours to see this great city. (Past participle of ride)

19. No one _____ the beauty of Washington, D.C. (Present of forget)

20. Many people have _____ their vacations in this city. (Past participle of spend)

44

Drill on Irregular Verbs

Name _____

In each of the following sentences, fill in the form of the irregular verb that is indicated.

We <u>bought</u> a basket of apples. (past of buy)

1. Many of us have _____ pictures of the Pilgrims. (past participle of see)
2. We _____ a little about their adventures. (present of know)
3. The Pilgrims _____ England on September 17, 1620. (past of leave)
4. One hundred and two people _____ England in search of freedom. (past of flee)
5. They _____ to America on the "Mayflower". (past of come)
6. They had _____ few belongings with them. (past participle of bring)
7. The voyage _____ two months and five days. (past of take)
8. The Pilgrims _____ an agreement about just laws. (past of make)
9. It was _____ as the Mayflower Compact. (past participle of know)
10. The Pilgrims _____ up their new homes. (past of set)
11. This _____ the colony of Plymouth. (past of begin)
12. The Pilgrims _____ to leave England for an important reason. (past participle of choose)
13. Freedom of worship _____ a great deal to them. (past of mean)
14. They _____ America as a new beginning. (past of see)
15. They _____ many hardships in this new land. (past of find)
16. The Pilgrims never _____ their problems in England. (past of forget)
17. This _____ them strong in their efforts. (past of keep)
18. They _____ hard against disease and starvation. (past of fight)
19. In the spring, the Mayflower _____ out for a return trip to England. (past of set)
20. The Pilgrims must have _____ homesick with the ship's departure. (past participle of feel)

45

Linking Verbs

> A linking verb couples or links a noun, pronoun or adjective to the subject in the sentence. The verb "be" and its various forms is the most common linking verb.

Underline the linking verb and circle the two words joined by that verb.

London is the capital of England.

1. A silkworm is a caterpillar of the silkworm moth.
2. Silk is a material from the silkworm.
3. It is a smooth material.
4. The textrure of the fabric is soft.
5. China is famous for its silk.
6. Silk-making is a complicated process.
7. Mulberry leaves are the diet of silkworms.
8. Healthy mulberry trees are important to the silk industry.
9. Silkworms are adult spinners 25 days after hatching.
10. About one-fifth of their weight is silk.
11. Silk is a thread from the silkworm's body.
12. Silk is the substance of the silkworm's cocoon.
13. The silk of a cocoon is one long unbroken thread.
14. The joining of the threads of several cocoons is a skill.
15. A skein is a coil of the silken threads.
16. For hundreds of years, silk was a luxury.
17. Silk was the most beautiful material for clothing.
18. Even today, silk is an important fabric.
19. It is a favorite fabric among many women.
20. Luxurious silks are sometimes multi-colored.

Linking Verbs

> A linking verb couples or links a noun, pronoun or adjective to the subject in the sentence. The verb **be** and its various forms is the most common linking verb.

Underline the linking verb and circle the two words joined by that verb.

The (capital) of the United States <u>is</u> (Washington, D.C.)

1. Four of the first five presidents were men from the state of Virginia.
2. Thomas Jefferson was one of them.
3. Monticello was the name of his home.
4. It is still a favorite tourist attraction in Virginia.
5. He was the third president of the United States.
6. He was famous early in our country's history.
7. Jefferson was a true patriot.
8. He was the author of the Declaration of Independence.
9. Thomas Jefferson was president from 1801 to 1809.
10. The United States was a small country during Jefferson's term in office.
11. A very large area of land was a purchase from France.
12. The area was land west of the Mississippi River.
13. It was land for new states.
14. Thomas Jefferson is famous for the purchase of the Louisiana Territory.
15. The Louisiana Purchase was important for the growth of our country.
16. Science and music were interests of Thomas Jefferson.
17. He was also a good architect.
18. Another interest of his was education.
19. He was the founder of the University of Virginia.
20. Thomas Jefferson was a really great American.

47

Transitive Verbs

> A transitive verb shows action passing from a doer to a receiver. A verb is transitive if it has a direct object or if it contains a form of the verb **be** plus a past participle.

Underline each transitive verb and circle the receiver of the action.

The workers <u>completed</u> the (job.)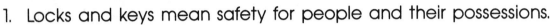

1. Locks and keys mean safety for people and their possessions.
2. Even the ancient Egyptions used locks.
3. Almost all locks have keys.
4. However, a combination lock has no key.
5. A person uses a combination of numbers for this type of lock.
6. Every lock has a bolt.
7. A key or knob moves the bolt.
8. Linus Yale invented the Yale lock in 1848.
9. The Yale lock needs a key.
10. The key moves little pins in the lock.
11. This frees the bolt.
12. Bank vaults have large combination locks.
13. The banker turns the knob on the combination lock to just the right numbers.
14. Only a few employees of the bank will know the combination.
15. Some vaults have time locks.
16. Clockworks in the lock make this setting possible.
17. Today almost every grown person carries several keys.
18. Keys open locks to houses and cars.
19. Some cars need two keys for operation.
20. This common use of locks protects property.

Transitive Verbs

> A transitive verb shows action passing from a doer to a receiver.

Underline each transitive verb and circle the receiver of the action.

Clarise <u>read</u> the (newspaper.)

1. Most people like plants.
2. They enjoy plants even in the winter.
3. Many people grow plants all year long.
4. Both men and women raise flowers.
5. Flower shops sell many potted plants.
6. Florists tell purchasers about proper care.
7. Proper sunlight helps plants.
8. Some plants require water every day.
9. Others need special plant food.
10. Some plants form beautiful leaves.
11. Certain plants produce blooms.
12. A grapefruit seed becomes a pretty plant.
13. Growers raise new violets from the old leaves.
14. People use small branches for new plants.
15. Many people grow plants as a hobby.
16. Many individuals keep plants in their homes.
17. Some people use greenhouses for indoor gardens.
18. Small indoor greenhouses are called terrariums.
19. I have several plants in my home.
20. My garden contains many flowers in the spring and summer.

Intransitive Verbs

An intransitive verb is one that has no receiver of its action. The subject is the doer of the action.

Underline the intransitive verb and circle the doer of the action.

Some (flowers) grow very well.

1. Many kinds of flowers grow in our gardens.
2. Some garden plants grow tall.
3. Many of the plants stand straight all by themselves.
4. Vines climb along fences or poles.
5. Some garden flowers live longer than others.
6. Some flowers live for two seasons.
7. A long growing season is needed for some flowers.
8. They must be planted early in the spring.
9. Some plants are raised indoors for a time.
10. Then they can be transplanted outdoors.
11. Often, petunias are started indoors.
12. Some flowers grow from seeds.
13. Many garden flowers are raised from bulbs.
14. Tulips grow from bulbs.
15. Certain types of soil are required for some plants.
16. Very rich soil is needed for sweet peas.
17. Zinnias will grow in poor soil.
18. However, they do not grow well in shade.
19. Today, flowers are being improved.
20. Growers are working for better varieties of garden flowers.

50

Intransitive Verbs

> An intransitive verb is one which has no receiver of its action. The subject is the doer of the action.

Underline the intransitive verb and circle the doer of the action.

The (storm) <u>struck</u> during the night.

1. Clouds form in the sky.
2. Moisture collects within the clouds.
3. These tiny water droplets join together.
4. Bigger drops are formed.
5. These drops of rain fall to the earth.
6. Sometimes the raindrops patter gently.
7. At other times, the rain beats heavily.
8. Actually, a cloud can not burst.
9. The amount of rainfall can be measured.
10. Rain gauges are used.
11. The gauges are read carefully.
12. Sometimes, the rain pours down.
13. A record was made in Holt, Missouri on June 22, 1947.
14. Twelve inches of rain fell in one hour.
15. Another record was established in 1911 in the Philippine Islands.
16. During a 24-hour period, 46 inches of rain fell.
17. On Mount Waialeali, nearly 470 inches of rain fall in a year.
18. Scientific experiments have been performed.
19. Certain experiments have worked well.
20. This study of rain will continue in the future.

Simple Tense

Tense indicates the time of the action or being. There are three simple tenses: present, past and future.

Present tense indicates action or being in present time.
Past tense indicates action or being in past time.
Future tense indicates action or being in future time.

The auxiliary verbs **will** and **shall** are used with the principal verb to form the future tense.

Underline the verb and tell whether it is in the present, past or future tense.

Present Jane writes poetry.
Past Jane wrote a poem.
Future Jane will write a poem for English class.

_____ 1. Some people call glaciers great sheets of ice.

_____ 2. Others refer to them as giant rivers of ice.

_____ 3. In the far north and south, glaciers will stretch to the sea.

_____ 4. Sometimes the ice pushes past the edge of the land.

_____ 5. Huge pieces of ice break from the glaciers.

_____ 6. Scientists named these floating glaciers icebergs.

_____ 7. One explorer compared the size of a southern iceberg to a 50-story building.

_____ 8. Another scientist measured a northern iceberg as more than 100 feet tall.

_____ 9. Many northern icebergs come from the icecap of Greenland.

_____ 10. Some icebergs float into warmer waters.

_____ 11. An iceberg will travel as far as 2000 miles.

_____ 12. All the colors of the rainbow will appear in an iceberg in the sunlight.

_____ 13. Ocean waves will cut caves in some icebergs.

_____ 14. In the past, icebergs presented problems to ships.

_____ 15. Researchers discovered the largest parts of icebergs below the surface of the water.

_____ 16. This hidden part spreads into a great shelf of ice.

_____ 17. An iceberg was the cause of the greatest shipwreck in this century.

_____ 18. An iceberg in the North Atlantic caused the destruction of the "Titanic".

Tense

Name _____

> Tense indicates the time of the action or being. There are three simple tenses: present, past and future.
>
>   Present tense indicates action or being in present time.
>
>   Past tense indicates action or being in past time.
>
>   Future tense indicates action or being in future time. The auxiliary verbs **will** and **shall** are used with the principal verb to form the future tense.

Underline the verb and tell whether it is in the present tense, past tense or future tense.

PRESENT   They <u>complete</u> their work.

PAST   They <u>completed</u> their work.

FUTURE   They <u>will complete</u> their work.

_____ 1. Scientists use microscopes to study tiny things.

_____ 2. A microscope enlarges things many times their normal size.

_____ 3. For example, particles of clay will look larger than usual.

_____ 4. Red cells from a person's blood will appear clearer in size and shape.

_____ 5. The word "microscope" came from the Greeks.

_____ 6. Many microscopes will have only one lens each.

_____ 7. Some microscopes will have more than one lens.

_____ 8. We called this type a compound microscope.

_____ 9. The lenses increase the appearance of objects.

_____ 10. The inventor of the microscope was probably a Dutch spectacle maker.

_____ 11. We know him as Zacharias Janssen.

_____ 12. He gave the Archduke of Austria a compound microscope in 1590.

_____ 13. Some doctors discovered important medical facts with a microscope.

_____ 14. Anton van Leeuwenhoek was a scientist in Holland 300 years ago.

_____ 15. He observed bacteria with a microscope.

_____ 16. He realized the importance of the microscope.

_____ 17. Today there are other kinds of microscopes.

_____ 18. Scientists discovered the planet, Pluto, with the Blink microscope.

Imperative Mood

> The imperative mood is used to express a command in the second person. In the imperative mood, the subject of the sentence is always **you,** either singular or plural. The subject word is rarely expressed.

Fill in the blanks with a verb in the imperative mood.

<u>Cut</u> the grass.

1. _____ the assignment carefully.
2. _____ the door quietly.
3. Always _____ distinctly.
4. _____ the table.
5. _____ the packages into the house.
6. _____ the seeds in the garden.
7. _____ the piano every day.
8. _____ the tickets for the concert.
9. Children, _____ your notes for the test.
10. _____ the doorbell.
11. _____ a good sport in all competitions.
12. _____ to the store for me, please.
13. _____ the flag in the morning.
14. Always _____ only the truth.
15. _____ your best manners.
16. _____ your name on the check.
17. _____ your bedroom on Saturday.
18. _____ the directions at the top of the page.
19. _____ the letters at the post office.
20. _____ the police in case of an emergency.

54

Agreement of Verb with Subject

Name _____

A singular subject needs a singular verb. A plural subject needs a plural verb. In most cases, the verb does not require a change in form to agree with its subject. However, in the third person of the present tense, the singular verb ends in **S**.

My friend **lives** near.
My friends **live** near.

Circle the correct verb form in each sentence below.

1. Erosion (is, are) the wearing away of land.
2. Wind, waves, ice and running water (does, do) most of the wearing away of land.
3. Wind-blown sand sometimes (carves, carve) rocks into strange shapes.
4. Waves also (wears, wear) away solid rock.
5. Rivers of ice (acts, act) like plows.
6. They (push, pushes) rocks and soil ahead of them.
7. These glaciers (gouges, gouge) deep valleys in the land.
8. Running water (is, are) the chief element in erosion.
9. Rainwater (does, do) more erosive damage than wind, waves and ice all together.
10. Loose soil (wears, wear) away faster than solid rock.
11. The Mississippi River (dumps, dump) tons of soil into the Gulf of Mexico each year.
12. Farmers (understands, understand) that erosion is the greatest enemy of their soil.
13. Erosion (occurs, occur) faster on soil without plant coverings.
14. A gully in a field (is, are) a danger sign.
15. Plant roots (helps, help) hold the soil in place.
16. Erosion (takes, take) place faster on hillsides than on level ground.
17. With this information, farmers (fight, fights) the effects of erosion.
18. They (plows, plow) fields on hillsides horizontally.
19. Today, people (knows, know) about the problem of erosion.
20. We (works, work) to prevent further damage to our valuable land.

Personal Pronouns

> A word used in place of a noun is a pronoun. A personal pronoun indicates the speaker, the one spoken to or the one spoken of.
>
> First person pronouns are: I, mine, me, we, ours and us.
> Second person pronouns are: you and yours.
> Third person pronouns are: he, she, it, his, hers, its, him, her, they, theirs and them.

Place the number 1 above pronouns of the first person, the number 2 above the pronouns of the second person, and the number 3 above pronouns of the third person.

        1
We will study a famous man.

1. Many of us have studied about Robert E. Lee.
2. We will study about him now.
3. He became a famous and respected man.
4. When Robert's father died, he was left to care for his invalid mother.
5. Whenever she was well enough, Robert took her for a drive in the country.
6. He became a West Point cadet at eighteen.
7. His family said they couldn't be prouder.
8. You can imagine the pride that was theirs.
9. He never received even one demerit at school.
10. I think that is remarkable.
11. At graduation, Lee's classmates said they admired him.
12. Whose school record is better, his or yours?
13. During the Mexican War, Lee showed us his great courage.
14. He played an important role in the Civil War.
15. It was the war between the North and South.
16. Lee loved this country of ours, but his loyalty fell with the South.
17. You can imagine how difficult it was for him to fight against the Union.
18. General Lee proved he was a great general, gaining many victories.
19. It is clear to me that General Lee was a man of honor.
20. We can respect him and the strength he showed.

Personal Pronouns

> The pronouns which denote the person spoken to are: **you** and **yours**.

In each of the following sentences, draw a circle around the pronoun which denotes the person spoken to.

Flying will be exciting for (you.)

1. Have you ever ridden in a airplane?
2. You will feel excitement when the plane takes off.
3. The first thing they tell you is to fasten your seat belts.
4. The flight attendant will make your flight comfortable.
5. This seat is yours.
6. Would you like something to drink?
7. Is this baggage yours?
8. You sometimes can see towns far below.
9. Do you have your ticket, sir?
10. The pilot will talk to you over the intercom.
11. He will let you know if you have to fasten your seat belts.
12. You may be served a meal.
13. There are magazines for you to read.
14. Some flights show movies for you to enjoy.
15. This book is yours to keep.
16. I've liked sitting next to you on the plane.
17. Yours was the best seat by the window.
18. The pilot will let you know when he is ready to land.
19. When the plane lands, take what is yours.
20. You will enjoy traveling by plane.

Number and Gender of Pronouns

Name _____

A singular pronoun replaces a singular noun. A plural pronoun replaces a plural noun.

The singular pronouns are: I, mine, me, you, yours, he, she, it, his, hers, its and him.

The plural pronouns are: we, ours, you, yours, they, theirs, us and them.

Underline the personal pronouns. Place an **S** above the singular pronouns and a **P** above the plural pronouns.

I saw them yesterday.

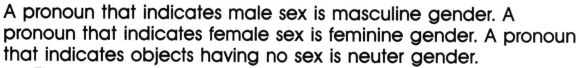

1. I love watching a parade.
2. She arrived with them an hour before it was to begin.
3. Can you girls hear the band playing?
4. They are marching down the street.
5. You may stand next to me for a better view.
6. Ours was the best place along the parade route.
7. One man in the parade sang songs for us.
8. He asked us to sing with him.
9. We enjoyed the clowns most of all.
10. It was a long parade, and we were tired when it ended.

A pronoun that indicates male sex is masculine gender. A pronoun that indicates female sex is feminine gender. A pronoun that indicates objects having no sex is neuter gender.

The masculine pronouns are: he, his and him.

The feminine pronouns are: she, hers and her.

The neuter pronouns are: it and its.

Plural pronouns may indicate all three genders.

Write a pronoun to take the place of each noun.

books – they

1. document
2. actress
3. Charles
4. keys
5. rabbit
6. sisters
7. boy
8. television
9. father
10. tourists
11. students
12. computer
13. nephew
14. journey
15. children
16. waiter
17. Victoria
18. tulips
19. program
20. Michael

Possessive Pronouns

> Pronouns used to indicate ownership or possession are called possessive pronouns.
> The possessive pronouns are: mine, yours, his, hers, its, ours and theirs.

Underline the possessive pronouns in the following sentences.

That book is <u>hers</u>.

1. The idea for this story is mine.
2. Have you thought about yours?
3. Hers is very interesting.
4. I wonder what his will be like?
5. Let's read theirs now.
6. The teacher helped me with mine.
7. Hers will not be finished until tomorrow.
8. The shortest stories were theirs.
9. Yours was the funniest story.
10. Ours was the best story time ever.

Interrogative Pronouns

> A pronoun used in asking a question is an interrogative pronoun.
> The interrogative pronouns are: who, what and which.
> **Who** is used in speaking of persons. **What** is used in speaking of things. **Which** is used in speaking of persons or things.
> Who is the only interrogative pronoun that changes form. Who is used as the subject or predicate nominative. When the sentence requires a direct object or an object of a preposition, use whom instead of who. The possessive form of this pronoun is whose.

Underline the interrogative pronouns in each sentence. Tell whether it refers to a person or a thing.

<u>Who</u> knew the answer?
^p

1. For whom will you vote?
2. Whom do you prefer?
3. What are the issues?
4. Which of you will speak first?
5. Which will be the moderator of the debate?
6. Who will count the ballots?
7. This ballot is mine, but whose is this?
8. Who was elected our class representative?
9. To whom will the title be awarded?
10. What are the results of the election?

Compound Personal Pronouns

Name _____

To form compound personal pronouns, add **-self** or **-selves** to certain forms of the personal pronouns.

First person compound personal pronouns are: myself and ourselves. Second person compound personal pronouns are: yourself and yourselves. Third person compound personal pronouns are: himself, herself, itself and themselves.

Underline the compound personal pronouns in the following sentences.

We helped <u>ourselves</u> to dessert.

1. The instructor said all students must prepare themselves for the examination.
2. He prepared himself for the test by studying carefully.
3. Are you, yourselves, ready?
4. We wrote the practice question ourselves.
5. I, myself, studied two hours.
6. Have you mastered the skills yourself?

Relative Pronouns

A relative pronoun is one that relates to a noun or pronoun which comes before it. The noun or pronoun that precedes the relative pronoun is called its antecedent.

The relative pronouns are: who, whom, which and that.

Who and **whom** relate to persons. **Which** relates to animals or things. **That** relates to persons, animals or things.

Underline the relative pronoun and circle its antecedent.

He could not attend the (schools) <u>that</u> were far away.

1. George Washington Carver was a boy who wanted to learn.
2. His life began as a slave who lived on a cotton plantation.
3. He was named after George Washington who was the first president.
4. The plantation owners gave the boy their own last name which was Carver.
5. After the war that freed the slaves, George remained with Mr. and Mrs. Carver.
6. George wanted an education which would help him in life.
7. Mrs. Carver gave him a Bible which he used as a reading textbook.

Uses of Pronouns (Subject)

Name _____

> Pronouns take the place of a noun. A pronoun may be used as the subject in a sentence.
> Subject pronouns: I, you, he, she, it, we, they.

Underline the subject pronouns.

<u>We</u> like gardening in our family.

1. In the spring, they planted the crops.
2. I tilled the ground on Saturday.
3. We fertilized the ground for them.
4. Now it was ready for planting.
5. She helped him place seeds in a row.
6. He covered the seeds with topsoil.
7. You must water the garden well.
8. Soon you will see tiny sprouts.
9. They will grow into larger sprouts.
10. Later he pulled the weeds from around the plants.
11. Now they will have more room to grow.
12. She checks on the plants every day.
13. I like to measure how much the plants have grown.
14. We put a scarecrow in the garden.
15. All day it scares away the birds.
16. We take our turns tending the garden.
17. He sprayed the garden for insects for my father.
18. Then I thinned out the rows of plants.
19. We grew delicious fruits and vegetables.
20. Soon we will harvest the crops.

Uses of Pronouns (Direct Object)

Name _____

> A pronoun may be used as the direct object of a verb.
> Object pronouns are: me, you, him, her, it, us, them.

Underline the object pronouns:

We saw <u>it</u> in the newspaper.

1. Six Flags Over Mid-America attracts me.
2. Erica likes it, too.
3. The rides thrill us every time we go!
4. The shows entertained us.
5. We saw them in the afternoon.
6. Have you ever seen them?
7. The actors picked her to come on stage.
8. She saw us in the audience.
9. The audience likes it very much.
10. The boys and girls cheered them.
11. The Time Tunnel scared us most of all.
12. The food satisfied him.
13. We lost her in line.
14. The police found her later.
15. A police dog helped them find her.
16. We wanted to reward it for helping.
17. That incident startled us!
18. It disturbed her and made her cry.
19. She followed us closely afterwards.
20. We enjoyed it anyway.

Predicate Pronouns

> A pronoun may be used as a predicate pronoun. A predicate pronoun follows a linking verb.
> The predicate pronouns are the same as the subject pronouns.

Draw a circle around the predicate pronoun in each sentence.

It was (I) who wrote this report.

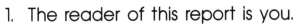

1. The reader of this report is you.
2. The first pilgrims were they.
3. The farmer is he.
4. After many months of travel, this was it.
5. The crop of corn was it.
6. The sick woman was she.
7. The most faithful man was he.
8. Was the captain he?
9. The doctor is he.
10. The leader of the Mayflower was he.
11. It was I who prepared the food on the ship.
12. The writer is she who kept notes during the voyage.
13. The happiest children were we in hopes of building a new home.
14. The first volunteers were they.
15. The best hunter was he.
16. "It is I!" exclaimed Governor Bradford.
17. It was the Indians and I who planted the corn.
18. The reader of the Bible was she.
19. It was I who farmed that plot of land.
20. The land of Plymouth Rock was it.

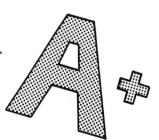

63

Descriptive Adjectives

Name _____

An adjective is a word used to describe or limit a noun or pronoun. An adjective that describes a noun or pronoun is called a descriptive adjective.

Underline the descriptive adjectives in these sentences.

The <u>small</u> dog ran down the <u>dark</u> street.

1. An earthquake is a frightening occurrence.
2. A mild earthquake may cause little damage.
3. Sometimes not even the tiniest damage is done.
4. A minor earthquake might simply rattle china cups on wooden shelves.
5. A severe earthquake can do an enormous amount of damage.
6. This would result in serious effects.
7. It may shake down tall buildings.
8. It could destroy an entire city.
9. A big earthquake at sea can trigger giant waves.
10. The worst earthquake in the United States occurred in 1906.
11. It destroyed a large portion of beautiful San Francisco.
12. Huge fires broke out because of this terrible earthquake.
13. Sometimes a volcanic eruption causes an earthquake.
14. An earthquake may also be caused by the sliding of huge masses of rock along a great crack in the earth.
15. Scientists invented a valuable instrument, a seismograph.
16. A seismograph can make an accurate record of an earthquake.
17. It can record both large and small earthquakes.
18. Clever engineers have designed special kinds of houses for dangerous areas.
19. These unique houses can make slight shifts during an earthquake.
20. Reinforced concrete is a good material for these houses.

Descriptive Adjectives

> An adjective is a word used to describe or limit a noun or pronoun. An adjective that describes a noun or pronoun is called a descriptive adjective.

Circle the descriptive adjectives and underline the nouns they modify.

The (small) girl read a (big) book.

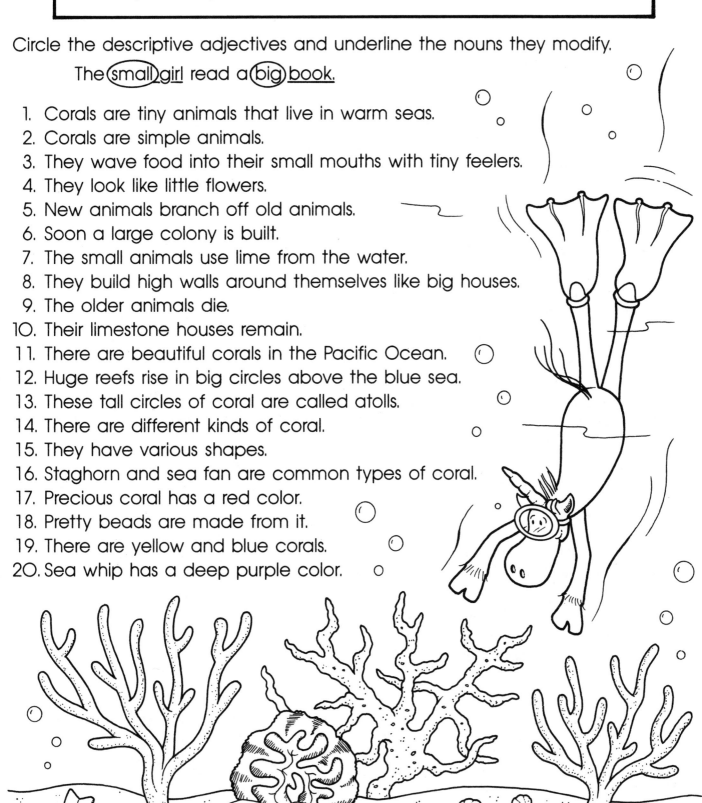

1. Corals are tiny animals that live in warm seas.
2. Corals are simple animals.
3. They wave food into their small mouths with tiny feelers.
4. They look like little flowers.
5. New animals branch off old animals.
6. Soon a large colony is built.
7. The small animals use lime from the water.
8. They build high walls around themselves like big houses.
9. The older animals die.
10. Their limestone houses remain.
11. There are beautiful corals in the Pacific Ocean.
12. Huge reefs rise in big circles above the blue sea.
13. These tall circles of coral are called atolls.
14. There are different kinds of coral.
15. They have various shapes.
16. Staghorn and sea fan are common types of coral.
17. Precious coral has a red color.
18. Pretty beads are made from it.
19. There are yellow and blue corals.
20. Sea whip has a deep purple color.

Positive Degree of Adjectives

Name _____

Adjectives change form according to the different degrees of comparison. There are three degrees of comparison: the positive, the comparative and the superlative.

The positive degree indicates quality.

In each sentence, underline the adjective in positive degree.

That is a <u>delightful</u> story.

1. Many people collect fine shells as a hobby.
2. The shell is the hard covering of some animals.
3. Shells make a good protection for the animals that have them.
4. The queen conch is a big shell.
5. This shell has a beautiful lining.
6. The lining has a smooth surface.
7. Some shells have round shapes.
8. Others have flat forms.
9. Other varieties have sharp edges.
10. It is possible to have a shell collection in a small place.
11. Some shells do not have large shapes.
12. Various types of shells have narrow contours.
13. Other shells would take up a great amount of space.
14. Animals with shells have lived in the deep sea for millions of years.
15. Many of the hard shells of these animals have sunk to the bottom of the sea.
16. They have formed thick layers in some places in the ocean.
17. Shells have been important possessions for humans at different times.
18. The American Indians used pretty shells for money.
19. Many tiny beads are made from shells.
20. Lovely buttons can also be made from shells.

Comparative Degree of Adjectives

Name _____

> The comparative degree indicates a greater or lesser degree of quality. It is used when comparing two items.

Form the comparative degree for each of the following adjectives.

Positive	Comparative
loud	louder
good	better

1. big
2. happy
3. useful
4. small
5. little
6. playful
7. kind
8. beautiful
9. large
10. important

Underline the adjectives in the comparative degree.

1. Vegetables are better in our diet than certain snacks.
2. Some vegetables are better sources of certain vitamins that others.
3. Vegetables are more valuable for providing minerals in the diet than some other types of foods.
4. Some vegetables are more delicious cooked.
5. Others are tastier raw.
6. Some vegetables, like squash, are more colorful than others.
7. Corn grows taller than many other vegetables.
8. Tomatoes are usually larger than radishes.
9. Today's methods for raising vegetables are more advanced than those of 100 years ago.
10. However, some vegetables are easier to grow than others.

Superlative Degree of Adjectives

Name _____

The superlative degree indicates the greatest or the least degree of quality. It is used when comparing three or more.

Form the comparative and superlative degrees for each adjective below.

Positive	Comparative	Superlative
light	lighter	lightest
good	better	best

1. much
2. tall
3. harmful
4. difficult
5. thoughtful
6. wide
7. helpful
8. dark
9. comfortable
10. bright

Underline the adjectives that are compared. Label if they are in the positive, comparative or superlative degree.

_____ 1. Most parts of the world have four seasons each year.

_____ 2. Summer is usually the hottest season.

_____ 3. Winter is the coldest time of the year.

_____ 4. Spring is generally warm.

_____ 5. In fall, the weather becomes cooler.

_____ 6. The earth is a farther distance from the sun in June than in December.

_____ 7. Summers would be warmer and winters colder in the northern hemisphere if that position were reversed.

_____ 8. People often give a simple reason for the changing of the seasons.

_____ 9. Scientific data offers a more complete explanation.

Limiting Adjectives

Name _____

A limiting adjective is one which points out an object or indicates number.

The articles are a, an and the. **The** is a definite article and is used with singular or plural nouns. **A** and **an** are indefinite articles. They are used with singular nouns.

Write the correct indefinite article before each noun.

_*a*_ teacher   _*an*_ author

1. _____ mountain
2. _____ advisor
3. _____ suitcase
4. _____ painting
5. _____ instrument
6. _____ storm

7. _____ forest
8. _____ umbrella
9. _____ example
10. _____ picnic
11. _____ machine

12. _____ award
13. _____ performance
14. _____ footprint
15. _____ hour
16. _____ contest

A numeral adjective is one which indicates an exact number such as six, forty or third.

In the following sentences, circle the articles and underline the numeral adjectives.

1. It is hard to imagine a time when there wasn't even one book.
2. The first books were made in Egypt more than five thousand years ago.
3. The first books were not made of pages bound together between a cover.
4. Sheets of papyrus were pasted together to form one long strip.
5. One strip was one hundred forty-four feet in length.
6. It took two hands to read such a roll book.
7. One hand-written book could take from six months to five years to copy.
8. Five hundred years ago, a book collector boasted all his books were "written with the pen".
9. Later, two inventions, paper and the printing press, changed the way books were made.
10. Recently, a collector paid five hundred thousand dollars for one copy of an early book printed on the Guttenberg press.

Demonstrative Adjectives

> **This, that, these** and **those** are adjectives that point out a definite person, place or thing. Use **this** and **these** to point out objects near at hand. Use **that** and **those** to refer to objects at a distance.

Use the proper demonstrative adjective before the following objects which are near at hand.

this camera   **these books**

1. _____ month	7. _____ paintings	13. _____ piano
2. _____ bicycle	8. _____ flag	14. _____ cars
3. _____ lamps	9. _____ girls	15. _____ dishes
4. _____ house	10. _____ shoes	16. _____ novel
5. _____ chairs	11. _____ peaches	17. _____ jobs
6. _____ team	12. _____ flowers	18. _____ boxes

Use the proper demonstrative adjective to point out the following objects which are at a distance.

that home   **those mountains**

1. _____ keys	7. _____ cabinets	13. _____ family
2. _____ city	8. _____ horse	14. _____ leaves
3. _____ buildings	9. _____ jars	15. _____ shelf
4. _____ jewels	10. _____ papers	16. _____ trees
5. _____ recipe	11. _____ journey	17. _____ playground
6. _____ plant	12. _____ games	18. _____ glasses

Indefinite Adjectives

An indefinite adjective is one that does not point out any one person, place or thing in particular.

The indefinite adjectives are: all, another, any, both, few, many, several, some, such and same.

Circle the indefinite adjective and underline the noun it modifies.

We had (some) fruit for dessert.

1. There are many kinds of jobs.
2. Both men and women have many choices open to them.
3. Any decision about a job takes careful thought.
4. Some jobs require special training.
5. Few jobs require no training.
6. Several occupations demand a college education.
7. Such requirements are necessary for doctors and lawyers.
8. Teachers also study for many years.
9. Counseling is another job.
10. This job requires several years of study and training.
11. All jobs involve some kind of mental or physical work.
12. Such labor provides several choices for workers.
13. Today's work force needs many kinds of people.
14. All workers should put forth much effort.
15. Choose your career from the many jobs available.
16. All kinds of opportunities await you.
17. Both education and enthusiasm are important factors.
18. Perhaps we will choose the same career.
19. We hope it will be more than just another job.
20. We anticipate much satisfaction in the job we choose.

Possessive Adjectives

> A possessive adjective is an adjective which indicates ownership.
> The possessive adjectives are: my, our, your, his, her, its and their.

Circle the possessive adjective and underline the noun it modifies.

These sentences are about (their) supplies.

1. His supplies are on her desk.
2. Their things had been lost for several days.
3. I keep my pencils in a case.
4. Keep your papers in a folder.
5. This will help keep your things organized.
6. Her book had several torn pages.
7. Its cover was dirty.
8. I hope her book is not ruined.
9. His pencil was missing its eraser.
10. A friend found their missing items.
11. My classmate shared her crayons with me.
12. Their pens were near your seat.
13. I was happy we could share our markers.
14. His bottle of glue is empty.
15. Sharpen your pencils now.
16. Their scissors are sharp.
17. Our reports are on her desk.
18. They passed their papers forward.
19. His project is not finished.
20. We store our books on the shelf.

Interrogative Adjectives

An interrogative adjective is one which is used in asking a question.
The interrogative adjectives are **what** and **which**.

Circle the interrogative adjective and underline the noun it modifies.

(Which) <u>boy</u> is first?

(What) <u>time</u> will you leave?

1. Which student will give the science report?
2. Which planet is farthest from the sun?
3. What type of heavenly body is the sun?
4. What planet is called the red planet?
5. What type of vegetation can be found on the moon?
6. Which planet is the largest?
7. What gases surround Jupiter?
8. Which star is the brightest in the night sky?
9. Which constellation includes the North Star?
10. What name is given to our galaxy?
11. What planet is encircled by rings?
12. From what language does the word "planet" come?
13. For which Roman god is Mars named?
14. What heavenly body is called Earth's satellite?
15. Which planets travel around the sun?
16. What planet do you live on?
17. On which heavenly body did man walk?
18. Which constellation is your favorite?

Write two more sentences using interrogative adjectives.

19. _____

20. _____

Predicate Adjectives

Name _____

Underline the linking verb and circle the predicate adjective.

The meal <u>was</u> (delicious.)

1. Many fruits and berries are edible.
2. They are necessary in the human diet.
3. Fruits are nutritious.
4. The vitamins in fruits are helpful.
5. Fruits and berries are red.
6. Others are yellow.
7. Many are purple.
8. The color is not important.
9. Some fruits and berries are sweet.
10. Others are sour to the taste.
11. Most are juicy.
12. Many fruits and berries are ripe in the spring.
13. Many varieties of apples are sweet.
14. Oranges are delicious.
15. Lemons are sour in taste.
16. Peaches, pears and plums are good.
17. Pineapples are tasty.
18. Cherries and grapes are popular as snacks.
19. Strawberries are common in desserts.
20. Fruits and berries are healthful.

Prepositions

> A preposition is a word used to show the relationship of a noun or a pronoun to some other word in a sentence.
> A preposition is placed before a noun or pronoun. This noun or pronoun becomes the object of the preposition.

Circle the preposition and underline its object.

The car raced (around) the <u>track</u>.

1. "Oh Susanna" and "My Old Kentucky Home" are two favorite songs in the United States.
2. They were written by Stephen Foster.
3. He wrote a number of other songs.
4. Many copies of his songs were sold.
5. However, he didn't make much money from them.
6. He died without a home.
7. Many friends forgot about him.
8. He died at a young age.
9. His songs lived after his death.
10. There are several memorials to Stephen Foster.
11. One memorial is in Pittsburgh.
12. Foster was born in Pittsburgh.
13. Pittsburgh is a city in Pennsylvania.
14. Another memorial is found along a riverbank.
15. The name of the river is Swannee.
16. The river was named in the song, "Old Folks at Home".
17. "My Old Kentucky Home" is the state song of Kentucky.
18. This song is sung before a famous horse race.
19. The Kentucky Derby is the name of the race.
20. Stephen Foster was a man of great talent.

Prepositions

A preposition is a word used to show the relationship of a noun or a pronoun to some other word in a sentence.

A preposition is placed before a noun or pronoun. This noun or pronoun becomes the object of the preposition.

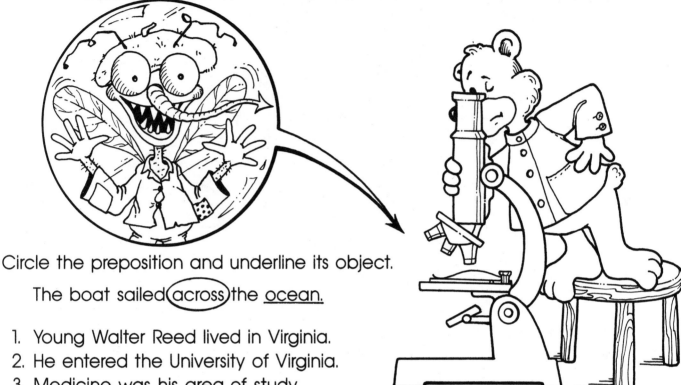

Circle the preposition and underline its object.

The boat sailed (across) the <u>ocean.</u>

1. Young Walter Reed lived in Virginia.
2. He entered the University of Virginia.
3. Medicine was his area of study.
4. He became the youngest medical graduate from the school.
5. Later, he became a doctor for the Army.
6. He was stationed in Arizona.
7. He doctored the soldiers of the garrison.
8. Reed also helped the other people in the region.
9. Fourteen years later, Reed was sent to Baltimore.
10. There he studied at John Hopkins University.
11. Soon he became a professor at the Army Medical School.
12. His experiments proved the reason for typhoid fever.
13. Germs from flies caused the disease.
14. Yellow fever was another problem for soldiers.
15. Reed and several other Army doctors went to Cuba.
16. They studied possible causes of the disease.
17. Their information pointed to mosquitoes.
18. Killing mosquitoes there brought an end to yellow fever.
19. This also worked in the United States.
20. Our government named a large army hospital for Walter Reed.

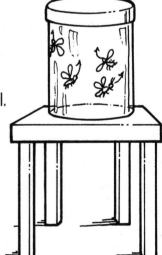

Adjectival Phrases

Name _____

An adjectival phrase is a group of words used as an adjective. The phrase begins with a preposition.

Underline the adjectival phrase and circle the noun it modifies.

An (evening) with shooting stars is exciting.

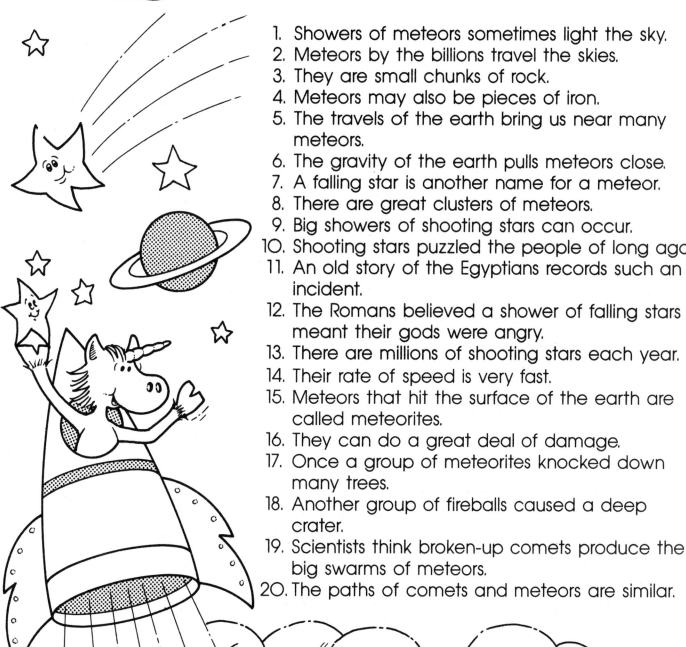

1. Showers of meteors sometimes light the sky.
2. Meteors by the billions travel the skies.
3. They are small chunks of rock.
4. Meteors may also be pieces of iron.
5. The travels of the earth bring us near many meteors.
6. The gravity of the earth pulls meteors close.
7. A falling star is another name for a meteor.
8. There are great clusters of meteors.
9. Big showers of shooting stars can occur.
10. Shooting stars puzzled the people of long ago.
11. An old story of the Egyptians records such an incident.
12. The Romans believed a shower of falling stars meant their gods were angry.
13. There are millions of shooting stars each year.
14. Their rate of speed is very fast.
15. Meteors that hit the surface of the earth are called meteorites.
16. They can do a great deal of damage.
17. Once a group of meteorites knocked down many trees.
18. Another group of fireballs caused a deep crater.
19. Scientists think broken-up comets produce the big swarms of meteors.
20. The paths of comets and meteors are similar.

Adjectival Phrases

> An adjectival phrase is a group of words used as an adjective. The phrase begins with a preposition.

Underline the adjectival phrase and circle the noun it modifies.

She has a large (collection) of shells.

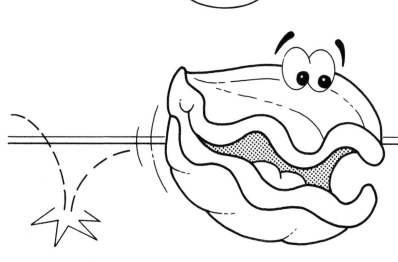

1. Marie Curie is an important name in science.
2. She was a girl of great intelligence.
3. Once, she received a gold medal for her good work.
4. She was a college student with little money.
5. Marie's life at college was difficult.
6. The desire for knowledge inspired her.
7. Pierre Curie was a scientist of great ability.
8. Their marriage began a partnership for a lifetime.
9. Long hours of hard work marked their years together.
10. The discovery of radium was recorded.
11. Eventually their work with radium was successful.
12. The discovery was a major breakthrough in scientific research.
13. The powerful effects of radium could help sick people.
14. Experiments with this element continued.
15. Many people of importance praised Pierre and Marie Curie.
16. Their dedication to science did not change.
17. Pierre's death was the end of their happy marriage.
18. Marie continued her experiments with radium.
19. Too much exposure to radium caused Marie's death.
20. The accomplishments of these two scientists will never be forgotten.

Adverbial Phrases

> An adverbial phrase is a group of words used as an adverb. A preposition begins an adverbial phrase.

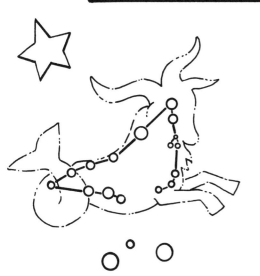

Circle the adverbial phrase and underline the verb it modifies.

Many cars <u>travel</u> (down this street.)

1. Many stars are seen in the night sky.
2. The stars are scattered across the sky.
3. They are in groups.
4. Ancient people saw pictures in the sky.
5. Most constellation names come from the Greeks and Romans.
6. Constellations appear in every direction.
7. Some constellations are visible in the United States.
8. These same constellations are never seen in some South American countries.
9. All constellations can be seen at the equator.
10. The night sky changes with the seasons.
11. It also changes with the earth's rotation.
12. The Big Dipper is always visible between the equator and the North Pole.
13. Fewer constellations disappear below the horizons in the far north.
14. A constellation may be visible in the western sky after sunset.
15. It will have set by midnight.
16. Other constellations will have risen in the east.
17. Stars move in different directions.
18. The constellations change in a slow progression.
19. Constellations change after many years.
20. The Big Dipper will have a different appearance in 100,000 years.

Adverbial Phrases

An adverbial phrase is a group of words used as an adverb. A preposition begins an adverbial phrase.

Circle the adverbial phrase and underline the verb it modifies.

Many people <u>live</u> (in Spain.)

1. Spain is located in southern Europe.
2. Spanish power increased with a wedding.
3. Princess Isabella and Prince Ferdinand married in 1469.
4. Columbus sailed under the Spanish flag.
5. He journeyed across the Atlantic Ocean.
6. The Spanish king and queen hoped for wealth.
7. New lands were claimed in 1492.
8. Great riches were brought from the New World.
9. The Spanish empire grew in size.
10. Spain's power decreased with the Navy's defeat.
11. Most Spanish colonies were lost by the nineteenth century.
12. Napolean ruled Spain for a time.
13. Spain has had many governments since Napoleon.
14. A revolt occured in 1936.
15. It was fought against the government.
16. A civil war raged in Spain.
17. This lasted for three years.
18. Francisco Franco became Spain's leader after the war.
19. Today there is a king in Spain once more.
20. Spain's progress has developed through the years.

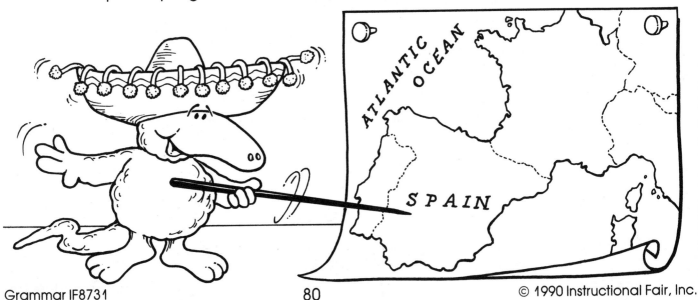

Adverbs of Time

> An adverb is a word that modifies a verb, an adjective or another adverb. Adverbs may indicate time, place or manner.
>
> Adverbs of Time answer the questions **when** or **how often**. They usually modify verbs.

Circle the Adverbs of Time and underline the verbs they modify.

My friends <u>meet</u> here (often.)

1. Today we will study about explorers.
2. Explorers often had hopes for great wealth and fame.
3. Voyages took place frequently in earlier times.
4. Leif Ericson reached North America first.
5. Later, Marco Polo traveled to Asia.
6. While in prison, he wrote almost daily about his travels.
7. His book about exploration was read frequently.
8. Columbus first sailed across the Atlantic in 1492.
9. He had already convinced the king and queen of Spain of the importance of the voyage.
10. The sailors soon became weary of the long voyage.
11. Later, Columbus made three other voyages.
12. He never reached the actual shores of North America.
13. Finally, Americus Vespucius sailed thousands of miles along the shores of the new continent.
14. Soon other explorers set out for the New World.
15. Next, John Cabot sailed to North America in 1497.
16. Missionaries soon arrived in the New World.
17. They immediately set out to educate the natives.
18. The exploration of space is now of great interest.
19. Have you ever thought about becoming such an explorer?

Tomorrow, you may explore new frontiers in space!

Adverbs of Time

> An adverb is a word that modifies a verb, an adjective or another adverb. Adverbs may indicate time, place or manner.
>   Adverbs of Time answer the questions **when** or **how often.** They usually modify verbs.

Circle the Adverbs of Time and underline the verbs they modify.

<u>Do</u> your homework (first.)

1. Today, we shall study lightning.
2. Lightning often skips from one cloud to another.
3. Then, it does no harm.
4. It frequently jumps from a cloud to the ground.
5. Suddenly, a serious problem can arise.
6. Sometimes, this results in damage or injury.
7. Occasionally, lightning will strike a house and set it on fire.
8. The common kind of lightning is usually called forked lightning.
9. Sheet lightning often appears low in the sky on summer evenings.
10. We shall study about ball lightning next.
11. It always looks like a ball of fire rolling along.
12. The ball finally explodes.
13. It then disappears from the sky.
14. This type of lightning is seldom seen.
15. Always observe the rules of safety concerning storms.
16. Never stand under a tree during a thunderstorm.
17. Move immediately to a proper shelter.
18. We already have learned some interesting facts about lightning.
19. Again, remember this helpful information.
20. It will never fail you.

Adverbs of Place

> **Adverbs of Place answer the question where.** They usually modify verbs.

Circle the Adverb of Place and underline the verbs they modify.

The kitten <u>darted</u> away.

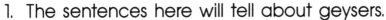

1. The sentences here will tell about geysers.
2. The eruption of a geyser sends forth gushes of water.
3. The geyser shoots water up into the air.
4. There must be hot rock not far below the ground.
5. A narrow, crooked passage must lead up from the hot rock.
6. The crooked passage is filled in with water.
7. Hot water is held here.
8. The boiling water at the bottom of the passage forms steam within.
9. The steam pushes out the cooler water at the top of the passage.
10. A little of this water comes out.
11. Then less cold water pushes down on the hot water.
12. Steam forms below.
13. The steam shoots the water upward.
14. The water soars above.
15. People must stand back.
16. Geysers are not formed everywhere around the world.
17. Old Faithful is found here in Yellowstone National Park.
18. It erupts there every 65 minutes.
19. Few people go away disappointed by the wait.
20. Other geysers are found far from the U.S. in Iceland and Greenland.

Adverbs of Place

> Adverbs of Place answer the question **where.** They usually modify verbs.

Circle the Adverbs of Place and underline the verbs they modify.

The dog ran away.

1. The sentences below are about lakes.
2. Lakes are located everywhere around the world.
3. Water runs in and out of fresh-water lakes.
4. Water runs down from the slope of the land.
5. The source of the water starts above.
6. Some large fresh-water lakes are here in our country.
7. Water flows in but not out of saltwater lakes.
8. Saltwater lakes are found here in dry regions.
9. One saltwater lake, the Caspian Sea, is far from the United States.
10. Water in lakes evaporates upward.
11. All salt in saltwater lakes stays there.
12. Plants spread out from the shores of some lakes.
13. Several lakes are situated high above sea level.

Fill in an Adverb of Place to complete each sentence. Use words from the list.

down	outside	overhead	there	away

1. You may play _____.
2. The bird flew _____.
3. The little girl fell _____.
4. The mailman left the package _____.
5. Fluffy clouds floated _____.

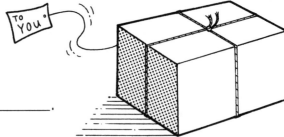

Adverbs of Manner

> Adverbs of Manner answer the question how or in what manner.
> They usually modify verbs.

Circle the Adverbs of Manner and underline the verbs they modify.

Drive the car carefully.

1. The game of baseball is easily considered the national sport of the United States.
2. In 1839, Abner Doubleday carefully laid out the first baseball diamond in Cooperstown, N.Y.
3. Baseball simply grew out of earlier types of games.
4. Baseballs and bats are made precisely.
5. They must fit the specifications of the rules exactly.
6. Players work hard during practice sessions.
7. They must run swiftly around the bases.
8. They also gracefully demonstrate many fielding skills.
9. These professionals play the game expertly.
10. Most people understand the game well.
11. People cheerfully await the beginning of the baseball season.
12. The fans cheer loudly for the team of their choice.
13. The game moves fast through nine innings.
14. Time passes slowly when the other team is winning.
15. At the end of the baseball season, the winners of the National League and the American League eagerly play the World Series.

Fill in an Adverb of Manner to complete each sentence. Use words from the list below.

quickly	carefully	neatly	bravely	kindly

1. Please arrange the books _____ on the shelves.
2. The ice cream melted _____ in the hot sun.
3. Always speak _____ to others.
4. The soldiers fought _____ for their country.
5. Do your work _____ at all times.

Comparison of Adverbs

> Many adverbs may be compared. They have three degrees of comparison: positive, comparative and superlative.

Complete each of the following comparisons.

POSITIVE	COMPARATIVE	SUPERLATIVE
fast	faster	fastest
bravely	more bravely	most bravely
much	more	most

1. far
2. quickly
3. hard
4. well
5. slowly
6. early
7. little
8. soon
9. badly
10. happily

Underline the adverbs and tell the degree of comparison.

_____1. Machines are used to do work easily.

_____2. Any type of machinery should be operated carefully.

_____3. A machine can do some work more efficiently than a person.

_____4. Some types of machinery are used to move objects more quickly.

_____5. A farmer uses a large combine to harvest his crops swiftly.

_____6. Computers can keep records most accurately.

_____7. With the development of machines, factories were built more hurriedly.

_____8. Cities grew fast.

_____9. Most probably people would not want to do without machines.

Correct Use of Adverbs

Name _____

> Adjectives modify nouns and pronouns. Adverbs modify verbs, adjectives or other adverbs. If the verb in the sentence is a linking verb, or if any form of the verb **be** can be substituted for the verb in the sentence, use an adjective. If the verb **be** cannot be substituted, use an adverb.

Choose the correct word in each sentence.

Daniel did the work (good, <u>well</u>)
His work is (<u>good</u>, well)

1. Justice is shown as a blindfolded woman (calm, calmly) holding a balance.
2. The reason for the scales is (easy, easily) to understand.
3. One must listen (careful, carefully) to both sides of a disagreement.
4. Justice must exercise fairness (complete, completely).
5. Since the beginning of man, some individuals have been treated (unfair, unfairly) by others.
6. Some early rulers settled disputes (clever, cleverly).
7. In ancient times, the leader of the tribe (usual, usually) decided guilt or innocence.
8. Certain stories of some early disputes are (true, truly).
9. One of these stories is about how King Solomon (wise, wisely) settled a question concerning a child.
10. King Solomon was (just, justly).
11. More than a few rulers became (famous, famously).
12. In many cases they acted (brave, bravely).
13. (Gradual, Gradually), courts of law came to settle disputes.
14. In many countries, courts are (full, fully) responsible for such decisions.
15. Judges and juries must be (honest, honestly).
16. They decide if a person is (guilty, guiltily).
17. This method is considered (good, well).
18. Deciding a case may not be (easy, easily).
19. Our courts (genuine, genuinely) work for justice for all.
20. The people's desire for justice is (great, greatly).

Interjections

An interjection is a word that **expresses strong emotion.**

Underline the interjection in each sentence.

1. Bravo! Here comes the parade.
2. Good! I can hardly wait.
3. That marching band is great. Wow!
4. The jugglers are next. Look!
5. Ah! The floats are beautiful.
6. Our school band is next. Hurrah!
7. Indeed! They played their best.
8. Ha! Ha! Watch the clowns.
9. That was quite a parade. Whew!
10. Good-bye! I'll meet you at school tomorrow.

Place an interjection before each sentence. Use the list below. Do not use a word more than once.

What	Ouch
Alas	Hush
Listen	Oh
Beware	Bah
Hello	Good

WOW!

1. _____! That step is shaky.

2. _____! I broke the vase.

3. _____! You must not talk now.

4. _____! Did we win the contest?

5. _____! I forgot my money.

6. _____! That is terrible.

7. _____! Is that you?

8. _____! I scraped my knee.

9. _____! I heard a noise.

10. _____! You arrived just in time.

Interjections

An interjection is a word that expresses strong emotion.

Underline the interjection in each sentence.

1. Oh! Here come the two teams.
2. Hush! The contest has begun.
3. Did you hear his answer? Listen!
4. Her answer was wrong. Alas!
5. Good! Our team is ahead.
6. That is a tricky question. Beware!
7. Great! Our team has one last chance.
8. That was good teamwork. Bravo!
9. Hurray! Our class won the contest.
10. Wow! The trophy is big.

Add an interjection before each sentence.

1. _____! It is raining hard.
2. _____! The baby is sleeping.
3. _____! That dog is dangerous.
4. _____! We won the baseball game.
5. _____! This rose is beautiful.
6. _____! The cold drink was refreshing.
7. _____! I thought I heard a noise.
8. _____! My name is Colleen.
9. _____! You completed the work.
10. _____! I'll see you later.

Conjunctions

Name _____

A conjunction is a word that joins words or groups of words in a sentence.

In each sentence, circle the conjunctions.

Gold (and) silver are valuable.
We may travel by plane (or) by train.
Christine went on the trip, (but) I stayed home.

1. Pine trees and fir trees are conifers.
2. Most conifers produce their seeds in cones or fruits.
3. Conifers can be trees or bushes.
4. Some junipers are short but hardy bushes.
5. The redwoods and sequoias are the giants of the plant world.
6. Conifers can be found in the United States and in other countries.
7. Unlike elms and maples, most conifers do not drop their leaves in winter.
8. Larches and bald cypresses are conifers.
9. They are conifers, but they are not evergreens.
10. Conifers can have scalelike leaves or narrow needles.
11. The needles can be different in length and in color.
12. They may be flat or four-sided in shape.
13. The needles may grow in bunches of two or more.
14. Millions and millions of conifers have been cut for lumber.
15. At Christmas time, conifers play a big part in our celebrations and decorations.
16. Many conifers have been killed by fires or disease.
17. Fires can occur by accident or on purpose.
18. We must plant and protect new trees.
19. They must be allowed to grow and mature.
20. Then there will be plenty of conifers and evergreens for the future.

90

Conjunctions

> A conjunction is a word that joins words or groups of words in a sentence.

In each sentence, circle the conjunction and underline the words or groups of words it connects.

We tell time by <u>hours</u> (and) <u>minutes</u>.
<u>Corn grows in Canada</u> (and) <u>in the United States</u>.
<u>They traveled to Florida</u>, (but) <u>we went to New York</u>.

1. Trade had its beginnings in marketplaces and at fairs.
2. Churches permitted buying and selling in their churchyards.
3. During the Middle Ages, Lords allowed markets and fairs to be held.
4. Peddlers and craftsmen sold their wares in these marketplaces.
5. Great fairs were held each year in cities and in towns.
6. The fairs at London and Stonebridge in England were famous.
7. Fairs were held in Paris and Lyons in France.
8. Spices and cloth were for sale along with the many other items.
9. The big fairs were held each year, but they were not held at the same time.
10. The fairs were gay and festive occasions.
11. Jugglers and fortune tellers made the fairs fun.
12. Fairs do not have the same importance or purpose they once had.
13. In the United States, there are many state and county fairs.
14. These fairs are important to farmers and ranchers.
15. Often clubs and schools have exhibits.
16. Carnival rides and races help everyone have a good time.
17. Vendors shout about the trinkets and foods for sale.
18. A world's fair may be held in one city or another.
19. Many countries send exhibits to show their progress in science or in art.
20. Displays in technology and industry are also of great interest.

Use of the Comma in a Series, with Dates and Geographic Names

Name _____

*Commas are used to separate words in a series.
>   The map shows cities, states, rivers and mountains.
>   Commas are used to set off parts of geographical names and dates.
>   Stephanie lived in St. Louis, Missouri.
>   Man landed on the moon on July 20, 1969.

Insert commas where they are needed in the following sentences.

1. The four largest countries in the world are Russia Canada China and the United States.
2. The Pilgrims landed in America in December 1620.
3. The Mississippi River flows into the Gulf of Mexico at New Orleans Louisiana.
4. Wheat corn rice and oats are kinds of cereals.
5. The United States declared independence on July 4 1776.
6. The Golden Gate Bridge is in San Francisco California.
7. Vegetable gardens may contain lettuce tomatoes beans and onions.
8. Baseball tennis and golf are popular summer sports.
9. The coldest day on record was August 24 1960 in Vostok Station Antarctica with a temperature of -127° Fahrenheit.
10. On September 22 1863 President Lincoln signed the Emancipation Proclamation.
11. Washington Adams Jefferson and Madison were the first four presidents.
12. Buckingham Palace is in London England.
13. Tulips roses lilies and daisies can be found in most flower gardens.
14. President John F. Kennedy was assassinated on November 22 1963.
15. Asia Africa Europe North America South America Australia and Antarctica are the seven continents.
16. The Constitution of the United States was adopted on September 17 1787.
17. Four basic operations in mathematics are addition subtraction multiplication and division.
18. The hottest day on record was September 13 1922 in Al' Aziziyah Libya with a temperature of 136° Fahrenheit.

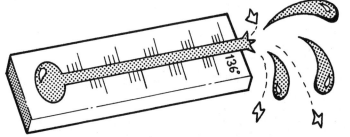

* In some textbooks, a comma is placed before the and.

Direct Quotations

Quotation marks are used before and after the exact words spoken by a person. Commas are used to set off short direct quotations, unless a quote is an interrogative or exclamatory sentence. Then a question mark or an exclamation point would be used after the quote.

> Mother said, "You may attend the game."
> "You may go," said Mother, "but be home for dinner."
> "What time is dinner?" Mike asked. "How much fun we had!" he exclaimed.

Supply quotations marks, commas, question marks or exclamation points when they are needed.

1. The librarian said Please be quiet.
2. Hush   scolded Father.
3. Can't you see that people are studying   he whispered.
4. I'm sorry I disturbed them   I said.
5. You should have known better   he said   than to talk out loud.
6. Where are the reference books   Father asked the librarian.
7. The woman replied   They are on the second floor.
8. Thank you   said Father.
9. Will you help me find the book I need   I asked him.
10. Yes   Father said   you can count on my help.
11. The sign says the reference section is to the left   I said.
12. You're right   he smiled.
13. We can sit at this table   I offered   when I write my report.
14. Father said   I'll read this book while you are working.
15. It's nearly time to leave   Father reminded me   because the library will be closing soon.
16. I'm almost finished with the assignment   I answered.
17. Thank you for your assistance   I said to the librarian as we left.
18. What a profitable trip to the library   Father remarked.

Synonyms

Name _____

> Synonyms are words that generally have the same meaning.

Match the synonyms in Column A with Column B.

Column A	Column B
___ 1. mercy	a tedious
___ 2. pity	b defend
___ 3. happy	c silly
___ 4. protect	d sympathy
___ 5. foolish	e risk
___ 6. tiresome	f associates
___ 7. sparkling	g compassion
___ 8. friends	h center
___ 9. employees	i glittering
___ 10. midst	j place
___ 11. catch	k cheerful
___ 12. put	l crowd
___ 13. peril	m companions
___ 14. dark	n grab
___ 15. group	o dim

funny

humorous

Fill in the blanks with pairs of words from above.

1. He showed me great _____ and _____ when I was feeling bad.

2. Mary was very _____ and _____ for riding on that wild horse.

3. The building was _____ and _____ .

4. The assignment was extremely _____ and _____.

5. We must _____ and _____ our rights at all times.

Antonyms

> ## Antonyms are words that mean the opposite.

Match the antonyms in Column **A** with Column **B**.

Column A		Column B	
____ 1. friend	**a**	innocent
____ 2. soldier	**b**	absent
____ 3. calm	**c**	civilian
____ 4. guilty	**d**	narrow
____ 5. dark	**e**	light
____ 6. present	**f**	bad
____ 7. full	**g**	enemy
____ 8. wide	**h**	empty
____ 9. good	**i**	quickly
____ 10. pretty	**j**	unruly
____ 11. slowly	**k**	cold
____ 12. answered	**l**	bright
____ 13. hot	**m**	ugly
____ 14. dull	**n**	descended
____ 15. barren	**o**	stale
____ 16. ascended	**p**	lazy
____ 17. fresh	**q**	asked
____ 18. ambitious	**r**	fruitful

Fill in the blanks with pairs of words from above.

1. A person should be considered _____ until proven _____.

2. It is better to have a person as a _____ than an _____.

3. If you are _____ instead of _____, you may not succeed.

4. The trees were _____ and not _____.

5. The entire class was _____ and not _____.

Synonyms and Antonyms

Name _____

Synonyms are words with the same or nearly the same meaning.

talk – speak

Antonyms are words which are opposite in meanings.

true – false   short – long

Match the pairs of synonyms by writing the letter of the word in Column **B** in front of the matching synonym in Column **A**.

Column A	Column B
____ empty	a. pardon
____ answer	b. concealed
____ excuse	c. reply
____ short	d. display
____ hire	e. collect
____ show	f. discovered
____ gather	g. employ
____ invented	h. large
____ hidden	i. vacant
____ great	j. brief

Match the pairs of antonyms by writing the letters of the word in Column **B** in front of its antonym in Column **A**.

Column A	Column B
____ wide	a. dull
____ before	b. noisy
____ quiet	c. idle
____ careful	d. cool
____ absent	e. take
____ warm	f. narrow
____ sharp	g. behind
____ give	h. present
____ wild	i. tame
____ busy	j. careless

Select the synonym for the words in parenthesis for each underlined word in the sentence.

1. The answer to the question was <u>wrong</u>. (right, incorrect, incomplete)
2. She is a <u>clever</u> girl. (pretty, silly, smart)
3. Baseball is an exciting <u>game</u>. (display, sport, show)
4. The doctor was <u>gentle</u> with the sick child. (kind, stern, impatient)
5. <u>Let</u> him help you with the problem. (request, ask, allow)

Select the antonym for the words in parenthesis for each underlined word in the sentence.

1. I always anticipate the <u>first</u> day of school. (opening, last, next)
2. This garden tool is <u>useful</u>. (helpful, broken, useless)
3. Put the package <u>there</u>. (near, here, away)
4. She usually arrives <u>early</u> for the show. (late, first, last)
5. He <u>always</u> completes his work on time. (almost, surely, never)

Homonyms

Homonyms are words that sound alike but differ in meaning.

Match the homonyms in Column **A** with Column **B**.

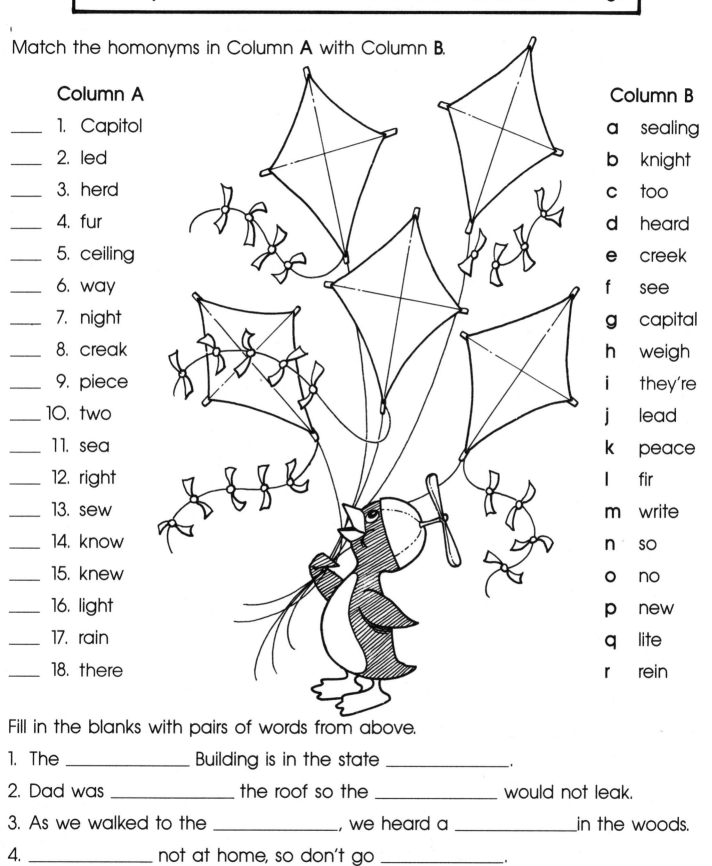

Column A		Column B	
___ 1. Capitol		**a**	sealing
___ 2. led		**b**	knight
___ 3. herd		**c**	too
___ 4. fur		**d**	heard
___ 5. ceiling		**e**	creek
___ 6. way		**f**	see
___ 7. night		**g**	capital
___ 8. creak		**h**	weigh
___ 9. piece		**i**	they're
___ 10. two		**j**	lead
___ 11. sea		**k**	peace
___ 12. right		**l**	fir
___ 13. sew		**m**	write
___ 14. know		**n**	so
___ 15. knew		**o**	no
___ 16. light		**p**	new
___ 17. rain		**q**	lite
___ 18. there		**r**	rein

Fill in the blanks with pairs of words from above.

1. The _____ Building is in the state _____.

2. Dad was _____ the roof so the _____ would not leak.

3. As we walked to the _____, we heard a _____ in the woods.

4. _____ not at home, so don't go _____.

5. The cattleman _____ his _____ of cattle moaning.

Homonyms

> Homonyms are words which sound alike but have different spellings and different meanings.

In the following sentences choose the correct homonym and write it in the blank.

Their house is around the corner from us. (their, there)

1. Last summer, we couldn't decide _____ to visit Boston or St. Louis. (weather, whether)

2. We chose to visit Boston, the _____ of Massachusetts. (capital, capitol)

3. We drove _____ the city in _____ days. (to, too, two)

4. Our _____ was over interstate highways. (route, root)

5. We _____ many signs along the way. (read, red)

6. My brothers couldn't hide _____ excitement. (their, there)

7. We found that _____ an exciting city. (its, it's)

8. It was interesting to _____ the accent of the people. (hear, here)

9. Many people related interesting _____ to us about the city's history. (tales, tails)

10. We appreciated the _____ and quiet of the parks. (peace, piece)

11. We walked up and down _____ of houses in the historic district. (rows, rose)

12. I wore a _____ in one of my shoes from _____ much walking. (whole, hole) (so, sew)

13. Luckily, this caused me _____ _____. (know, no) (pain, pane)

14. I had to have the _____ of the shoe repaired. (soul, sole)

15. My family did little sightseeing at _____ . (night, knight)

16. We were able to _____ souvenirs at a _____ . (buy, by) (sail, sale)

17. _____ entire family enjoyed the trip. (our, hour)

18. This was a _____ vacation. (great, grate)

19. We only spent _____ days _____. (fore, four) (they're there)

20. _____ you like to go, _____? (would, wood) (to, too, two)

Contractions

Name _____

A contraction is a shortened form of two or more words. An apostrophe is used in a contraction to show where a letter or letters have been left out.

Write the words from which these contractions are made:

1. they're _____
2. can't _____
3. hasn't _____
4. it's _____
5. won't _____
6. doesn't _____
7. wouldn't _____
8. you'll _____
9. we've _____
10. don't _____

Write the contractions for the following words:

1. have not _____
2. of the clock _____
3. there is _____
4. are not _____
5. we will _____
6. were not _____
7. I am _____
8. did not _____
9. you are _____
10. I shall _____

Use the contraction doesn't when referring to one person, place or thing.
Use the contraction don't when referring to more than one and with the words I and you.
He doesn't understand the direction.
I don't know the way.

Cross out the incorrect word in parenthesis.

1. Our vacation (don't, doesn't) begin until tomorrow.
2. They (don't, doesn't) expect to do much sightseeing.
3. She (don't, doesn't) have a camera to take pictures of her trip.
4. The shuttle bus to the plane (don't, doesn't) hold many people.
5. You (don't, doesn't) have to hurry.
6. I (don't doesn't) like to rush through the airport.
7. The noise of the jets (don't, doesn't) bother me.
8. (Don't, Doesn't) worry about the baggage.
9. They hope the suitcases (don't, doesn't) arrive until they have checked into customs.
10. That plane (doesn't, don't) land at this airport.

Compound Words

> Some words are made by putting two words together. They form a compound word.
>
> water + melon = watermelon

Match a word from **Column A** with a word in **Column B** to make a compound word. Write the new word on the line below.

Column A

1. box	9. play
2. in	10. home
3. ground	11. sail
4. rail	12. him
5. pea	13. foot
6. soft	14. tooth
7. sun	15. water
8. water	16. over

Column B

road	ache
mate	work
ski	boat
side	cock
loose	shine
self	ball
car	ride
ball	fall

1. _____

2. _____

3. _____

4. _____

5. _____

6. _____

7. _____

8. _____

9. _____

10. _____

11. _____

12. _____

13. _____

14. _____

15. _____

16. _____

ANT + EATER = ANTEATER

Capital Letter Review

Name _____

In the sentences below, circle the words that should begin with a capital letter.

(have) you been to (new orleans, louisiana?)

1. louisiana is a state in the deep south.
2. its nickname is the pelican state.
3. some refer to it as the nation's sugar bowl.
4. louisiana was named after louis XIV.
5. he was king of france nearly 300 years ago.
6. louisiana has many tourist attractions.
7. creole food is very good to eat.
8. vieux carre is the french quarter.
9. new orleans is below sea level.
10. baton rouge is the capital.
11. new orleans is a popular city.
12. mardi gras is a special time.
13. most of the land is fertile.
14. did you know the french settled louisiana?
15. they were followed by the spaniards.
16. after the revolutionary war british colonists settled there.
17. most people today are american-born.
18. french customs and traditions remain alive.
19. many plantations are still in use.
20. most of the people in southern louisiana are roman catholic.

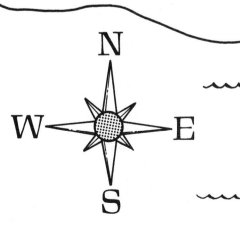

Punctuation Review

Name _____

Put the correct form of punctuation in the following sentences.

Insects frighten me.

1. An insect is a small animal
2. It is an invertebrate animal which means it has no spine
3. Did you know every insect has three parts
4. These parts are the head thorax and abdomen
5. Biting insects have strong jaws
6. Insects pollinate flowers
7. Do you like to catch insects
8. The honeybee provides us with honey
9. Wow Silkworms spin thread
10. How many insects are there
11. More than 800,000 different species have been described
12. Moths butterflies ants bees wasps and flies are just a few
13. Some insects lay eggs
14. Many produce in large numbers
15. Are you allergic to bees
16. Yes I am
17. I love to catch butterflies
18. My bug collection is fantastic
19. The word bug is a slang word
20. Insects benefit us

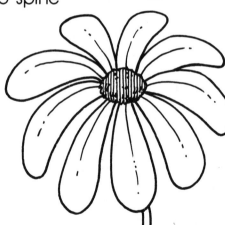

Answer Key

Page 1

Sentences   Name _____

> A sentence is a group of words which express a complete thought.

Write S before each group of words that is a **sentence**. Write N before each group of words that is not a sentence.

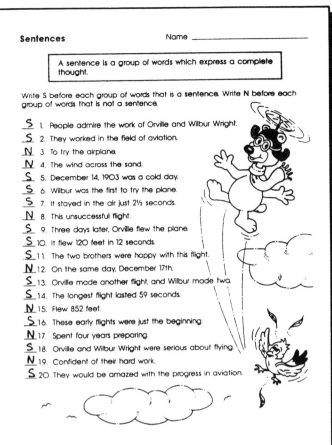

- S 1. People admire the work of Orville and Wilbur Wright.
- S 2. They worked in the field of aviation.
- N 3. To try the airplane.
- N 4. The wind across the sand.
- S 5. December 14, 1903 was a cold day.
- S 6. Wilbur was the first to try the plane.
- S 7. It stayed in the air just 2½ seconds.
- N 8. This unsuccessful flight.
- S 9. Three days later, Orville flew the plane.
- S 10. It flew 120 feet in 12 seconds.
- S 11. The two brothers were happy with this flight.
- N 12. On the same day, December 17th.
- S 13. Orville made another flight, and Wilbur made two.
- S 14. The longest flight lasted 59 seconds.
- N 15. Flew 852 feet.
- S 16. These early flights were just the beginning.
- N 17. Spent four years preparing.
- S 18. Orville and Wilbur Wright were serious about flying.
- N 19. Confident of their hard work.
- S 20. They would be amazed with the progress in aviation.

Page 2

Recognition of Sentences   Name _____

> A sentence is a group of words which express a complete thought.

Write S in the blank if it is a complete thought and NS if it is not a complete thought.

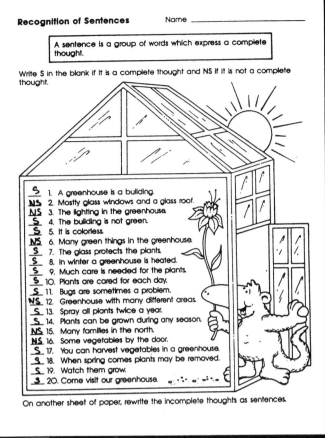

- S   1. A greenhouse is a building.
- NS 2. Mostly glass windows and a glass roof.
- NS 3. The lighting in the greenhouse.
- S   4. The building is not green.
- S   5. It is colorless.
- NS 6. Many green things in the greenhouse.
- S   7. The glass protects the plants.
- S   8. In winter a greenhouse is heated.
- S   9. Much care is needed for the plants.
- S 10. Plants are cared for each day.
- S 11. Bugs are sometimes a problem.
- NS 12. Greenhouse with many different areas.
- S 13. Spray all plants twice a year.
- S 14. Plants can be grown during any season.
- NS 15. Many families in the north.
- NS 16. Some vegetables by the door.
- S 17. You can harvest vegetables in a greenhouse.
- S 18. When spring comes plants may be removed.
- S 19. Watch them grow.
- S 20. Come visit our greenhouse.

On another sheet of paper, rewrite the incomplete thoughts as sentences.

Page 3

Subject of the Sentence   Name _____

> The subject is that part of a sentence that names a person, a place or a thing about which a statement is made. It may be a noun or pronoun.

Underline the subject in the following sentences.

This <u>report</u> is about Central America.

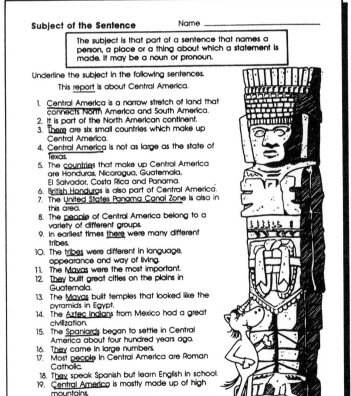

1. <u>Central America</u> is a narrow stretch of land that connects North America and South America.
2. <u>It</u> is part of the North American continent.
3. <u>There</u> are six small countries which make up Central America.
4. <u>Central America</u> is not as large as the state of Texas.
5. The <u>countries</u> that make up Central America are Honduras, Nicaragua, Guatemala, El Salvador, Costa Rica and Panama.
6. <u>British Honduras</u> is also part of Central America.
7. The <u>United States Panama Canal Zone</u> is also in this area.
8. The <u>people</u> of Central America belong to a variety of different groups.
9. In earliest times <u>there</u> were many different tribes.
10. The <u>tribes</u> were different in language, appearance and way of living.
11. The <u>Mayas</u> were the most important.
12. <u>They</u> built great cities on the plains in Guatemala.
13. The <u>Mayas</u> built temples that looked like the pyramids in Egypt.
14. The <u>Aztec Indians</u> from Mexico had a great civilization.
15. The <u>Spaniards</u> began to settle in Central America about four hundred years ago.
16. <u>They</u> came in large numbers.
17. Most <u>people</u> in Central America are Roman Catholic.
18. <u>They</u> speak Spanish but learn English in school.
19. <u>Central America</u> is mostly made up of high mountains.
20. The <u>people</u> live in the high areas because it's always like spring.

Page 4

The Complete Subject   Name _____

> The person, the place or thing about which a statement is made is called the simple subject or the subject. A simple subject with all its modifiers is called the complete subject.

Underline the complete subject.

<u>People from many states</u> visit the St. Louis Zoo.

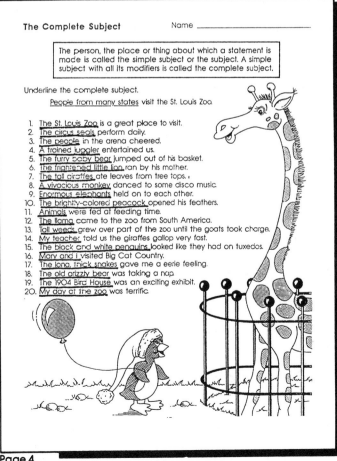

1. <u>The St. Louis Zoo</u> is a great place to visit.
2. <u>The circus seals</u> perform daily.
3. <u>The people</u> in the arena cheered.
4. <u>A trained juggler</u> entertained us.
5. <u>The furry baby bear</u> jumped out of his basket.
6. <u>The frightened little lion</u> ran by his mother.
7. <u>The tall giraffes</u> ate leaves from tree tops.
8. <u>A vivacious monkey</u> danced to some disco music.
9. <u>Enormous elephants</u> held on to each other.
10. <u>The brightly-colored peacock</u> opened his feathers.
11. <u>Animals</u> were fed at feeding time.
12. <u>The llama</u> came to the zoo from South America.
13. <u>Tall weeds</u> grew over part of the zoo until the goats took charge.
14. <u>My teacher</u> told us the giraffes gallop very fast.
15. <u>The black and white penguins</u> looked like they had on tuxedos.
16. <u>Mary and I</u> visited Big Cat Country.
17. <u>The long, thick snakes</u> gave me a eerie feeling.
18. <u>The old grizzly bear</u> was taking a nap.
19. <u>The 1904 Bird House</u> was an exciting exhibit.
20. <u>My day at the zoo</u> was terrific.

Answer Key

Predicate of the Sentence   Name _____

> The predicate is that part of a sentence that tells something about the subject. All sentences must contain a predicate which is always a verb. The most important part of any sentence is the predicate.

Circle the predicate in each sentence.

A trip to British Columbia (is) a great experience.

1. British Columbia (is) the western-most province in Canada.
2. Early settlers (came) from Great Britain.
3. Most people of today (are) Canadian-born.
4. The people (work) in a variety of industries.
5. They (work) in sawmills, fish canneries and wood factories.
6. The lumberjacks (cut) wood in the great northern forests.
7. Many people (farm) the land.
8. British Columbia (ranks) third in the production of copper, gold and coal.
9. The Anglican church (is) the largest in British Columbia.
10. British Columbia (is) extremely mountainous.
11. British Columbia (has) a warmer climate than the other Canadian provinces.
12. Captain James Cook (landed) on Vancouver Island more than 175 years ago.
13. They (exchanged) goods for furs.
14. Gold (was discovered) in this area in 1858.
15. Today British Columbia (ships) products all over the world.
16. It (was) difficult to build a railroad because of the high mountains.
17. Trade (flourished) and cities (grew) rapidly.
18. The lumber industry grew rapidly.
19. The water route from Vancouver to Alaska (is) one of the most beautiful trips in the world.
20. There (are) many attractions to visit in British Columbia.

Page 5

The Complete Predicate   Name _____

> The simple predicate with all its modifiers is called the complete predicate.

Underline the complete predicate.

The study of ancient Greece <u>would be interesting.</u>

1. Did you know the ancient Greeks <u>wrote many plays?</u>
2. The history of Greece <u>goes back for thousands of years.</u>
3. The earliest record <u>shows the beginning of Greece in 776 B.C.</u>
4. The Greek civilization <u>came to its climax in 450 B.C.</u>
5. The expanding Roman Empire <u>overshadowed Greece.</u>
6. The ancient Greeks <u>did not have a single government.</u>
7. They <u>lived in separate city-states.</u>
8. Early Greeks <u>lived in low houses.</u>
9. The public buildings in a Greek city <u>were most beautiful.</u>
10. Most of the public buildings <u>were temples to gods.</u>
11. The Greeks <u>worshiped many gods.</u>
12. The Greeks <u>built the first open-air theater.</u>
13. All of the characters <u>were played by men.</u>
14. The Greeks <u>loved athletics.</u>
15. The best athletes <u>would meet every four years in Olympia.</u>
16. Ancient Greece <u>was the center of science.</u>
17. Many early Greeks <u>gave much wisdom to the world.</u>
18. In ancient Greece, many wars <u>were fought between the city-states.</u>
19. The Greeks <u>taught the Romans much about art and literature.</u>
20. The history of ancient Greece <u>was ended in 1453.</u>

Page 6

Compound Predicates   Name _____

> A sentence may have a compound predicate. A conjunction connects the compound predicate of a sentence.

Underline the compound predicate and circle the conjunction which connects them.

You <u>read</u> (and) <u>remember</u> your homework.

1. We will <u>read</u> (and) <u>study</u> about insects.
2. Insects <u>live</u> (and) <u>reproduce</u> nearly all over the world.
3. Many insects <u>live</u> (and) <u>die</u> within a relatively short period of time.
4. Some insects <u>develop</u> (and) <u>grow</u> in four stages.
5. Other insects <u>hatch</u> (and) <u>emerge</u> from their eggs looking like the adult insects.
6. Some insects <u>grow</u> (and) <u>shed</u> their skins several times during their life cycles.
7. Some types of insects <u>live</u> (and) <u>work</u> in big insect societies.
8. Experts <u>identified</u> (and) <u>labeled</u> the three body parts of insects.
9. All insects <u>have</u> (and) <u>use</u> six legs and one pair of feelers.
10. Some insects <u>crawl</u> (or) <u>hop.</u>
11. Other insects <u>jump</u> (or) <u>walk.</u>
12. Most insects <u>walk</u> (or) <u>fly.</u>
13. Many insects <u>possess</u> (and) <u>use</u> wings as their chief means of movement.
14. Some <u>can fly</u> (and) <u>glide</u> through the air for considerable distances.
15. Most insects <u>inhale</u> (and) <u>exhale</u> air.
16. Tiny tubes <u>receive</u> (and) <u>send</u> air to all parts of their bodies.
17. Air <u>enters</u> (and) <u>reaches</u> the tubes through tiny holes called spiracles.
18. Scientists <u>classified</u> (and) <u>grouped</u> the hundreds of thousands of insects into various orders.

Page 7

Subject and Predicate   Name _____

> The subject is the part of the sentence that tells the person, place or thing about which the statement is made.
> The predicate is the part of the sentence that tells something about the subject.

Circle the subject and underline the verb in each sentence.

1. (Charlotte Bronte) <u>wrote</u> the book, <u>Jane Eyre.</u>
2. (Emily Bronte) <u>wrote</u> the book, <u>Wuthering Heights.</u>
3. The two (sisters) <u>lived</u> in Yorkshire, England.
4. These (girls) <u>suffered</u> tragedies and poor health.
5. The (sisters) <u>wrote</u> stories as a relief from their problems.
6. (Charlotte) <u>wrote</u> <u>Jane Eyre</u> from a woman's point of view.
7. The (book) <u>broke</u> with traditional writing.
8. The (heroine) of the story <u>was</u> a realistic character.
9. The (book) <u>grew</u> in appreciation through the years.
10. (Emily Bronte) <u>polished</u> her writing ability.
11. This (writer) <u>placed</u> her deep feelings in the characters of her story.
12. (Emily) <u>was</u> a shy girl.
13. The (girl) <u>avoided</u> people outside her own family.
14. (Writing) <u>was</u> an outlet for Charlotte and Emily Bronte.
15. The (sisters) <u>became</u> famous.
16. Their two (books) <u>are</u> masterpieces.
17. Many (people) <u>read</u> their books.
18. The (novels) <u>hold</u> a high place in literature.

Page 8

Answer Key

Review on Complete Subject and Complete Predicate

Name _____

Underline the Complete Subject with one line and the Complete Predicate with two lines.

The country of Germany is very old.

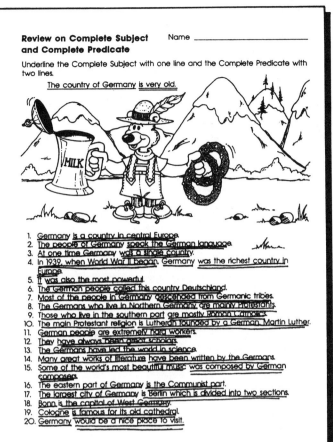

1. Germany is a country in central Europe.
2. The people of Germany speak the German language.
3. At one time Germany was a single country.
4. In 1939, when World War II began, Germany was the richest country in Europe.
5. It was also the most powerful.
6. The German people called this country Deutschland.
7. Most of the people in Germany descended from Germanic tribes.
8. The Germans who live in Northern Germany are mainly Protestants.
9. Those who live in the southern part are mostly Roman Catholics.
10. The main Protestant religion is Lutheran founded by a German, Martin Luther.
11. German people are extremely hard workers.
12. They have always been great scholars.
13. The Germans have led the world in science.
14. Many great works of literature have been written by the Germans.
15. Some of the world's most beautiful music was composed by German composers.
16. The eastern part of Germany is the Communist part.
17. The largest city of Germany is Berlin which is divided into two sections.
18. Bonn is the capital of West Germany.
19. Cologne is famous for its old cathedral.
20. Germany would be a nice place to visit.

Page 9

Declarative Sentences

Name _____

A declarative sentence states a fact.

Circle the words that should be capitalized. Punctuate each sentence.

(our) body is truly incredible.

1. The human body is like a machine.
2. Its working parts can do useful work.
3. Your body needs food and oxygen.
4. The human body is very complex.
5. Man could never build anything this complex.
6. The body is made up of flesh, blood and bones.
7. The bones form the skeleton.
8. The skeleton is the framework on which the body is built.
9. Your skeleton is joined together to keep the body firm.
10. The human body is about three-quarters water.
11. Some important substances are calcium, phosphorus and carbon.
12. Food that you eat must be organic matter.
13. Some parts of the food are stored in the body.
14. Our lungs take in oxygen.
15. The heart is a mighty pump.
16. The body is protected by an outside covering called skin.
17. Man is capable of reasoning because of his brain.
18. Humans have the ability to reproduce.
19. Our bodies can overcome diseases.
20. We must take care of all our parts.

Page 10

Imperative Sentences

Name _____

An imperative sentence is one that gives a command.
Put the dishes on the table.

Pick out the imperative sentences from the following list. Write the name imperative on the line in front of those sentences. Do not mark in the spaces before the other types of sentences.

1. Would you like to go on a camping trip?
2. Living close to nature can be fun.
Imperative 3. Plan such trips carefully.
Imperative 4. Choose a campsite suitable to your interests.
5. Some people like to fish or hunt.
6. Others like to swim or hike.
7. Have you ever gone canoeing on a camping trip?
8. It is important to bring the necessary equipment for a camping trip.
Imperative 9. Pack the supplies with care.
Imperative 10. Bring comfortable and durable clothes.
11. Blankets and sleeping bags are necessary.
Imperative 12. Pack foods that are not easily spoiled.
Imperative 13. Don't forget the pots, pans, dishes and utensils.
Imperative 14. Never leave behind your compass and first aid kit.
Imperative 15. Look for a safe and convenient area for the tent.
Imperative 16. Set up the tent properly.
17. It will be your home on the trip.
18. Did you follow the directions carefully?
Imperative 19. Check to make sure the campfire is out before leaving the campsite.
20. Many forest fires have been caused by careless campers.

Page 11

Interrogative Sentences

Name _____

An interrogative sentence asks a question.

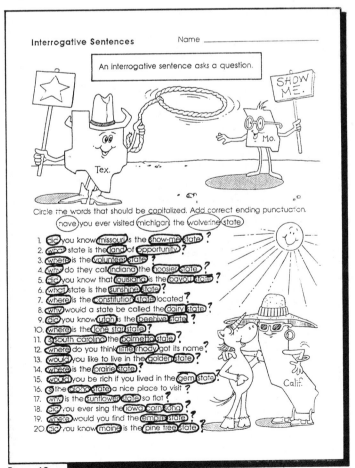

Circle the words that should be capitalized. Add correct ending punctuation.

(have) you ever visited (michigan) the (wolverine state)?

1. Did you know missouri is the show-me state?
2. What state is the land of opportunity?
3. Where is the volunteer state?
4. Why do they call indiana the hoosier state?
5. Did you know that louisiana is the bayou state?
6. What state is the sunshine state?
7. Where is the constitution state located?
8. Why would a state be called the dairy state?
9. Did you know utah is the beehive state?
10. Where is the lone star state?
11. Is south carolina the palmetto state?
12. Where do you think little rhody got its name?
13. Would you like to live in the golden state?
14. Where is the prairie state?
15. Would you be rich if you lived in the gem state?
16. Is the aloha state a nice place to visit?
17. Why is the sunflower state so flat?
18. Did you ever sing the iowa corn song?
19. Where would you find the empire state?
20. Did you know maine is the pine tree state?

Page 12

Answer Key

Exclamatory Sentences   Name _____

> An exclamatory sentence is one that expresses strong emotion.
> Sometimes interrogative and exclamatory sentences begin with similar words.

Identify the sentences. Write exclamatory, interrogative or imperative on the lines. Place the correct punctuation mark after each sentence.

What a wonderful surprise!

interrog. 1. Have you ever been in a cavern?
exclamatory 2. How large the cave is!
interrog. 3. What forms such big caves?
interrog. 4. How are large caverns formed?
exclamatory 5. What an amazing feat of nature!
interrog. 6. How far are we below the surface of the ground?
interrog. 7. How are different rooms formed within a cave?
imperative 8. Be careful as you walk through the cavern.
imperative 9. Don't get separated from the rest of the group.
exclamatory 10. What thick walls divide the rooms of the cave!
exclamatory 11. What beautiful icicles hang from the roof of the cavern!
interrog. 12. How were these stone icicles named stalactites?
interrog. 13. What are the names of the stone icicles growing up from the floor of the cave?
interrog. 14. How many years does it take to form stalactites and stalagmites?
exclamatory 15. How pretty are the colors of the stone icicles!
interrog. 16. What forms the flower-like crystals on the walls?
exclamatory 17. How delicate these shapes appear!
exclamatory 18. How interesting caves are!
exclamatory 19. How I enjoyed my first trip through a cave!
imperative 20. Come with me on my next trip.

Page 13

Types of Sentences   Name _____

> A declarative sentence states a fact. It is followed by a period.
> An interrogative sentence asks a question. It is followed by a question mark.
> An imperative sentence gives a command. It is followed by a period.
> An exclamatory sentence expresses sudden or strong emotion. It is followed by an exclamation point.

Label each type of sentence. Place the proper punctuation mark at the end.

declarative 1. There are twelve months in a year.
interrogative 2. Can you name the months in order?
imperative 3. Write the names of the months on your paper.
exclamatory 4. What beautiful handwriting this is!
declarative 5. Our vacation time is during the summer months.
interrogative 6. Are you planning a trip for this summer?
exclamatory 7. What a great time we had last year!
imperative 8. Tell me about your experiences on the trip.
declarative 9. We toured the western United States.
declarative 10. Our first stop was the Grand Canyon.
exclamatory 11. How high the canyon walls stand!
interrogative 12. Have you ever visited the Grand Canyon?
declarative 13. We spent part of our vacation camping in Colorado.
interrogative 14. Do you like to camp?
exclamatory 15. What a memorable time we had last summer!
declarative 16. We spend nearly nine months of the year in school.
declarative 17. This time is spent learning many new things.
declarative 18. A good education will open new opportunities for us.
imperative 19. Write a composition about this school year.
exclamatory 20. How quickly the year seems to pass!

Page 14

Simple and Compound Sentences   Name _____

> A simple sentence contains one subject and one predicate.
> Colleen collects foreign stamps.
> A compound sentence contains two independent sentences which are closely related. A conjunction usually joins the two clauses of a compound sentence.
> The wind blew hard, and the rain poured down.

Label each sentence below as a simple or a compound sentence. In the compound sentences, circle the conjunction which joins the clauses.

Simple 1. Many children fly kites for fun.
Compound 2. We don't know who invented the kite, (but) the Chinese used a flat kite 2000 years ago.
Compound 3. The Chinese enjoy flying kites very much, (and) they have a national holiday called Kites' Day.
Simple 4. Kites have meant a great deal to the people of China, Japan and Korea.
Simple 5. Even grown-ups fly kites in these countries.
Compound 6. Kites are used as toys, (but) they have been used for other purposes, too.
Simple 7. The ancient Chinese flew kites to drive away evil spirits.
Simple 8. Weather Bureaus have used kites to send weather instruments high into the air.
Simple 9. A kite played an important part in a very famous experiment.
Compound 10. Benjamin Franklin flew a kite during a thunderstorm, (and) he discovered that lightning was a spark of electricity.
Simple 11. Ordinary flat kites must have tails.
Compound 12. The tail weighs down the lower end, (and) this helps to keep the kite from nose-diving.
Simple 13. Box kites do not need tails.
Simple 14. Many kites are brightly decorated.
Simple 15. The Chinese sometimes attach streamers to their kites.
Simple 16. Wind is needed for kite flying.
Simple 17. A day with gentle breezes is best for kite flying.
Compound 18. It is fun to fly kites, (and) they are interesting to watch.

Page 15

Use of Capital Letters and Periods   Name _____

> Use a capital letter for the first word of every sentence, all proper nouns and proper adjectives. Capitalize initials and abbreviations when capitals would be used if the words were written in full.
> Place a period after declarative and imperative sentences, abbreviations and initials.

Circle each letter which should be a capital and place periods where they are needed.

1. Only one man has been the president of the U.S. for more than two terms.
2. His parents were James and Sara D. Roosevelt.
3. His name was Franklin D. Roosevelt.
4. The family lived in New York.
5. After graduating from Harvard University, he attended Columbia Law School.
6. He married a distant cousin, Eleanor Roosevelt.
7. They had five children, Anna, James, Elliot, Franklin and John.
8. Roosevelt was asked by President Woodrow Wilson to work in Washington, D.C.
9. In 1928, Roosevelt was elected governor of New York.
10. Four years later, he became the 32nd U.S. president.
11. By the time Roosevelt had finished his second term, World War II was underway.
12. On Dec. 7, 1941 the Japanese attacked Pearl Harbor.
13. This attack brought the U.S. into the war.
14. The American people were unwilling to change presidents during such a time.
15. Old Roosevelt was re-elected to a third term.
16. He lead the United States of America through many months of the war.
17. Not surprisingly, F.D.R. was chosen for a fourth term in office.
18. However, he didn't live to see the end of World War II.
19. He died on Apr. 12, 1945 in Warm Springs, Georgia.
20. Franklin D. Roosevelt has been honored by Americans and other people around the world.

Page 16

Answer Key

Recognizing Nouns   Name _____

A noun is a word which names a person, place or thing.
person: girl, policeman, neighbor
place: kitchen, city, zoo
thing: desk, pen, fence

The words below are nouns. Write each one in the proper column to show whether it names a person, place or thing.

	Person	Place	Thing
1. voters	voters		
2. United States		United States	
3. lawyer	lawyer		
4. cabin			cabin
5. America		America	
6. year			year
7. Abraham Lincoln	Lincoln		
8. speech			speech
9. theater			theater
10. president	president		

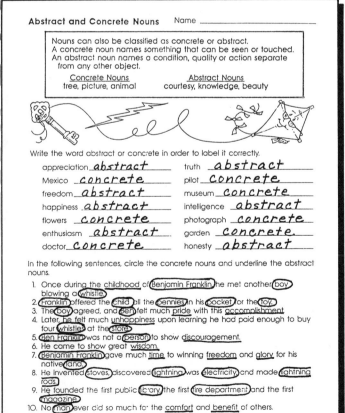

Underline the nouns in each sentence:
1. Abraham Lincoln was born in Kentucky.
2. He lived with his mother, father and sister in a small cabin.
3. During his childhood, Abraham did not often attend a school.
4. Later his family moved to Indiana and then to Illinois.
5. Abraham Lincoln worked as a clerk and then became a lawyer.
6. He was elected a congressman for the state of Illinois.
7. Abraham Lincoln became the President of the United States in the year 1861.
8. The Civil War was fought while Lincoln was president.
9. Lincoln gave his famous speech, the Gettysburg Address, in November of 1863.
10. In April, 1865, John Wilkes Booth shot the president as he watched a play at Ford's Theatre in Washington, DC.

Proper and Common Nouns   Name _____

A proper noun names a particular person, place or thing.
A common noun names any one of a class of persons, places or things.

Columbus Finds America

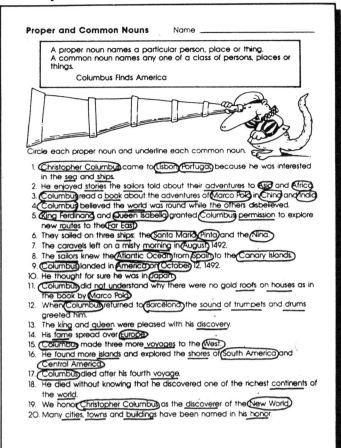

Circle each proper noun and underline each common noun.
1. Christopher Columbus came to Lisbon, Portugal because he was interested in the sea and ships.
2. He enjoyed stories the sailors told about their adventures to Asia and Africa.
3. Columbus read a book about the adventures of Marco Polo in China and India.
4. Columbus believed the world was round while the others disbelieved.
5. King Ferdinand and Queen Isabella granted Columbus permission to explore new routes to the Far East.
6. They sailed on three ships: the Santa Maria, Pinta and the Nina.
7. The caravels left on a misty morning in August, 1492.
8. The sailors knew the Atlantic Ocean from Spain to the Canary Islands.
9. Columbus landed in America on October 12, 1492.
10. He thought for sure he was in Japan.
11. Columbus did not understand why there were no gold roofs on houses as in the book by Marco Polo.
12. When Columbus returned to Barcelona, the sound of trumpets and drums greeted him.
13. The king and queen were pleased with his discovery.
14. His fame spread over Europe.
15. Columbus made three more voyages to the West.
16. He found more islands and explored the shores of South America and Central America.
17. Columbus died after his fourth voyage.
18. He died without knowing that he discovered one of the richest continents of the world.
19. We honor Christopher Columbus as the discoverer of the New World.
20. Many cities, towns and buildings have been named in his honor.

Abstract and Concrete Nouns   Name _____

Nouns can also be classified as concrete or abstract.
A concrete noun names something that can be seen or touched.
An abstract noun names a condition, quality or action separate from any other object.

Concrete Nouns	Abstract Nouns
tree, picture, animal	courtesy, knowledge, beauty

Write the word abstract or concrete in order to label it correctly.

appreciation	abstract	truth	abstract
Mexico	concrete	pilot	concrete
freedom	abstract	museum	concrete
happiness	abstract	intelligence	abstract
flowers	concrete	photograph	concrete
enthusiasm	abstract	garden	concrete
doctor	concrete	honesty	abstract

In the following sentences, circle the concrete nouns and underline the abstract nouns.
1. Once during the childhood of Benjamin Franklin, he met another boy blowing a whistle.
2. Franklin offered the child all the pennies in his pocket for the toy.
3. The boy agreed, and Ben felt much pride with this accomplishment.
4. Later he felt much unhappiness upon learning he had paid enough to buy four whistles at the store.
5. Ben Franklin was not a person to show discouragement.
6. He came to show great wisdom.
7. Benjamin Franklin gave much time to winning freedom and glory for his native land.
8. He invented stoves, discovered lightning was electricity and made lightning rods.
9. He founded the first public library, the first fire department and the first magazine.
10. No man ever did so much for the comfort and benefit of others.

Persons of Nouns   Name _____

Person is the quality of a noun through which the speaker, the one spoken to, or the one spoken about is indicated.
1. The first person refers to the speaker.
2. The second person refers to the one spoken to.
3. The third person refers to the one spoken about.

On the line before each sentence, write the person of the underlined noun.
3 1. The Declaration of Independence was signed on July 14, 1776.
1 2. We, Americans, were given many freedoms through this document.
2 3. Students, have you seen the document at the Smithsonian Institute?
3 4. Yes, our class visited this museum last May.
3 5. In 1775, the Continental Congress was formed.
3 6. The representatives met the following year to continue their efforts towards independence.
1 7. We, colonists, wanted complete freedom from England.
3 8. The Declaration of Independence told why the colonies wanted to be free.
2 9. Class, do you know the reasons why we wanted our freedom?
2 10. Pupils, do you know the wrongs that were suffered by the colonists?
3 11. The Declaration of Independence stated the colonies would become an independent nation.
3 12. Thomas Jefferson did most of the writing with the help of John Adams and Benjamin Franklin.
1 13. We, citizens, are indebted to these men and those who signed.
3 14. Fifty-six men signed the Declaration.
1 15. We, countrymen, have greatly benefited from the Declaration of Independence.

© 1990 Instructional Fair, Inc.

Answer Key

Page 21

Persons of Nouns

Name _____

> Person is the quality of a noun through which the speaker, the one spoken to, or the one spoken about is indicated.
> The first person refers to the speaker.
> The second person refers to the one spoken to.
> The third person refers to the one (person, place or thing) spoken about.

On the line before each sentence, write the person of the underlined noun.

3 1. One way of telling a <u>story</u> is to present it as a stage performance.
3 2. Such a performance is called a <u>play</u>.
2 3. <u>Children</u>, have you ever seen a play?
3 4. Plays are usually given in a <u>theater</u>.
1 5. We, the <u>audience</u>, must watch and listen carefully.
3 6. The first theaters were built by the ancient <u>Greeks</u>.
3 7. During the Middle Ages, the <u>people</u> of Europe became interested in acting.
3 8. Many of the plays at this time told <u>stories</u> from the Bible.
3 9. During the time of <u>William Shakespeare</u> no women acted in plays.
2 10. <u>Boys</u>, have you ever thought of performing on stage?
1 11. We, <u>girls</u>, now have the opportunity to become actresses.
3 12. Today, much acting is done before a <u>camera</u> instead of an audience.
3 13. Many actors appear on <u>television</u>.
3 14. A really great <u>actor</u> makes us forget who he is while performing.
1 15. We, the <u>listeners</u>, concentrate only on the part he is playing.
3 16. The actor allows us to understand the <u>character</u> in the play.
3 17. We can also understand the <u>emotions</u> felt by the character.
3 18. Acting is now thought of as an <u>art</u>.
1 19. We, <u>Americans</u>, pay great actors as much honor as we pay great painters or musicians.
2 20. <u>Ladies</u> and <u>gentlemen</u>, let's have a round of applause for this play.
3 21. The theater and acting are always a thrill for us <u>spectators</u>.

Page 22

Number

Name _____

> Number is the quality of a noun which indicates whether it refers to one person, place or thing, or more than one.
> A singular noun denotes one person, place or thing.
> A plural noun denotes more than one person, place or thing.
>
> | Singular Nouns | | Plural Nouns | |
> |---|---|---|---|
> | bat | box | bats | boxes |
> | picture | gas | pictures | gases |
> | apple | peach | apples | peaches |

Write S for singular and P for plural of the following nouns.

P dishes   P patches
S porch   S radio
S house   P sons
P pencils   S teacher
P axes   S soldier
P knives   S cup

Underline the following nouns. Place S above the singular nouns and P above the plural nouns.

1. California has a coastline stretching along the Pacific Ocean for more than 1,000 miles.
2. The Spanish first settled this area, followed by the Mexicans.
3. California became the 31st state in 1850.
4. Pioneers headed for California in the 1840's to look for gold.
5. Newcomers found the region very pleasant.
6. California farmers and fishermen lead the states in the dollar value of their products.
7. The most valuable crop in California is cotton; followed by citrus fruits.
8. The lowest land in the United States is found in California. It is known as Death Valley.
9. There are four national parks in California.
10. This state is an interesting place for people to visit.

Page 23

Number of Nouns

Name _____

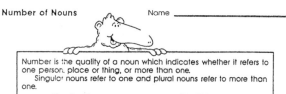

> Number is the quality of a noun which indicates whether it refers to one person, place or thing, or more than one.
> Singular nouns refer to one and plural nouns refer to more than one.
>
> | Singular Nouns | | Plural Nouns | |
> |---|---|---|---|
> | suggestion | hero | suggestions | heroes |
> | wish | sheep | wishes | sheep |
> | half | man | halves | men |
> | colony | | colonies | |

Write each of the following words in the proper column and form the matching singular or plural noun.

	Singular	Plural			Singular	Plural
1. trick	trick	tricks	8. child	child	children
2. life	life	lives	9. shelves	shelf	shelves
3. echo	echo	echoes	10. cities	city	cities
4. curtains	curtain	curtains	11. attorney	attorney	attornys
5. classes	class	classes	12. porch	porch	porches
6. deer	deer	deer	13. feet	foot	feet
7. duty	duty	duties	14. countries	country	countries

Underline the nouns in the following sentences and label each as singular or plural. Place an S above the singular nouns and a P above the plural nouns.

1. There are mountains that shoot out streams of hot rock and ashes.
2. These mountains are called volcanoes.
3. People of long ago made up stories to explain them.
4. Each volcano forms in much the same way.
5. Gases deep in the earth force molten rock through an opening in the ground.
6. The red-hot rock that pours from volcanoes is called lava.
7. When lava cools into solid rock, it forms piles around the opening.
8. In time, the piles become a cone-shaped mountain.
9. At the top of the volcanic cone is a hollow called a crater.
10. Volcanoes can build themselves on land or rise from the bottom of oceans and seas.

Page 24

Gender of Nouns

Name _____

> Gender is the quality of a noun through which sex is indicated. There are three genders: masculine which denotes the male sex, feminine which denotes the female sex and neuter which denotes objects which have no sex.
> A noun that may be either masculine or feminine is usually considered masculine unless otherwise noted in the context of a sentence.
>
> | Masculine Gender | Feminine Gender | Neuter Gender |
> |---|---|---|
> | husband | wife | home |
> | waiter | waitress | table |

Label each noun according to the correct gender.

1. grandfather M   9. newspaper N
2. heroine F   10. aunt F
3. queen F   11. heir N
4. carpet N   12. princess F
5. nephew M   13. umbrella N
6. statue N   14. sister F
7. actress F   15. stallion M
8. emperor M   16. encyclopedia N

Underline the nouns in the following sentences and label each according to its gender. Place an M above the nouns denoting masculine gender, F above the nouns denoting feminine gender, and N above the nouns denoting neuter gender.

1. Dolly Payne was a little girl who lived in Virginia during the Revolutionary War.
2. When she grew up, she married James Madison.
3. He became the fourth President of the United States.
4. They lived in the new city built on the banks of the Potomac River.
5. This city was named after George Washington.
6. The president and his wife shared a new home called the White House.
7. A valuable painting of George Washington hung in the dining room.
8. During the War of 1812, English soldiers marched through the streets of the city.
9. Before they reached the capital, Dolly placed the famous picture in her carriage.
10. This brave lady left behind her own belongings.
11. Dolly Madison became one of the best-loved women in American history.

Answer Key

Grammar IF8731

Page 25

Nouns Used as Subjects and Predicate Nominatives

Name _____

> Case is the quality of a noun that shows its relationship to some other word in the sentence. There are three cases: nominative case, possessive case and objective case.
> A noun used as the subject of a verb is in the nominative case.

Draw a line under the nouns used as subjects in the following sentences.

A sudden <u>storm</u> appeared on the horizon.

1. Many <u>stories</u> have been written about Paul Bunyan.
2. Once, a blue <u>snow</u> fell in his North Woods.
3. The forest <u>animals</u> fled farther north.
4. Some <u>bears</u> became polar bears.
5. <u>Paul</u> discovered a blue calf during the storm.
6. The big <u>man</u> cared for the calf named Babe.
7. Soon the <u>calf</u> grew very large.
8. <u>Babe</u> became Paul's constant companion.
9. <u>News</u> about Paul and Babe traveled far.
10. <u>Paul Bunyan</u> was known as the greatest logger of all time.

> A noun used as a predicate nominative is in the nominative case. The noun that follows a linking verb and refers to the same person or thing as the subject is the predicate nominative.

In the following sentences, underline the subject and circle the predicate nominative.

The <u>winner</u> of the contest is (Mary.)

1. "Gulliver's Travels" is a famous (story.)
2. The <u>author</u> is (Jonathan Swift.)
3. The <u>book</u> is a (story) of adventure.
4. A long sea <u>voyage</u> was the (setting.)
5. The <u>land</u> of Lilliput was not the planned (destination.)
6. The main <u>character</u> was (Gulliver.)
7. This <u>voyager</u> was now a (prisoner) in Lilliput.
8. Later, the <u>man</u> was the (friend) of the emperor.
9. Many <u>Lilliputians</u> were (helpers) in preparing for Gulliver's departure.
10. The <u>seafarer</u> was an (Englishman) returned home at last.

Page 26

Direct Address

Name _____

> A noun used in direct address is in the nominative case.
> Sharon, please close the door.

Underline the noun in direct address.

Where are the keys, <u>John</u>?

1. <u>Erika</u>, when was New Orleans founded?
2. The city was begun in 1718, <u>Megan</u>.
3. For forty years, <u>Anthony</u>, the city was controlled by the French.
4. Then the French turned it over to the Spanish, <u>Jones</u>.
5. <u>Sammy</u>, the Spanish held the city for thirty years and then gave it back to the French.
6. The French, <u>Charles</u>, then sold it to the United States as part of the Louisiana Purchase.
7. New Orleans is on delta land built by the Mississippi River, <u>Robert</u>.
8. <u>Mary</u>, New Orleans was an important port from its beginning.
9. Ocean vessels, <u>Jason</u>, could sail up the river to it.
10. Riverboats can reach it easily, <u>Lori</u>.
11. <u>Mark</u>, the very first steamboat on the Mississippi was named the "New Orleans".
12. Today, <u>Kyle</u>, New Orleans is a city of more than half a million people.
13. <u>Rebecca</u>, it is still a leading southern port of the United States.
14. Tourists visit New Orleans, <u>Shawna</u>, by the thousands.
15. Each year, during the week before Lent, <u>Melissa</u>, the city has a carnival.
16. This carnival is called the Mardi Gras, <u>Nicholas</u>.
17. It is the gayest festival in all the United States, <u>Sue</u>.
18. <u>Jane</u>, one part of the celebration is a grand parade down Canal Street.
19. At Mardi Gras time, <u>Latriece</u>, visitors crowd into the streets.
20. <u>Christie</u>, these visitors help make New Orleans a prosperous city.

Page 27

Appositives in the Nominative Case

Name _____

> A noun in apposition is in the same case as the noun it explains.
> A noun in apposition with the subject or predicate nominative is in the nominative case.

Underline the appositive and circle the word it explains.

Tom (Dooley,) a doctor, treated the sick.
This is my (cousin) Donald

1. One (man,) Leonardo DaVinci, represents civilization during the Renaissance.
2. (DaVinci,) the painter, was also the first engineer of his time.
3. (Andrea del Verrocchio,) a famous artist, was Leonardo's tutor.
4. DaVinci's patron was (Lodovico Sforza,) the Duke of Milan.
5. A (patron,) the artist's employer, assigned the projects to be completed.
6. The (projects,) oil paintings, were requested by the Duke.
7. (Leonardo,) the observer, kept many books of notes and drawings.
8. These (notes,) scientific observations, were not translated into English until the late 1800's.
9. (DaVinci,) a genius, was not truly appreciated for hundred of years.
10. Leonardo was also an (astronomer,) a gazer of stars.
11. (Leonardo,) the architect, designed an elaborate revolving stage.
12. This great man was also an aeronautical (engineer,) a designer of flying machines.
13. The spring-driven (helix,) the first helicopter, was his invention.
14. A military (engineer,) DaVinci, designed advanced war machines.
15. One such (machine,) an armored tank, was well ahead of the times.
16. (Botany,) the study of plants, also interested Leonardo DaVinci.
17. It is (DaVinci,) the artist, that is most admired.
18. A (painting,) the "Mona Lisa", is surrounded by legends.
19. The (Last Supper,) a masterpiece, is best known.
20. This (mural,) his greatest creation, was badly damaged.

Page 28

Use of Comma with Words in Direct Address and Apposition

Name _____

> A comma is used to set off words in direct address.
> Clean your room, Jill.
> Jill, put your things in order.
> Clean your room, Jill, and put your things in order.

Insert commas to show the words in direct address.

1. Today, students, we will discuss inventors.
2. Joan, do you know who invented the telephone?
3. Alexander Graham Bell was the inventor, Rose.
4. No one is really sure who invented the printing press, Nichole.
5. Some people believe, class, that it was invented by Johann Geutenberg.
6. Kari, another important inventor was Thomas Edison.
7. Were you aware, Jimmy, that he invented the phonograph?
8. Robert, the television does not have a single inventor.
9. Three people are credited with its development, Melissa.
10. Their names, boys and girls, are Vladimir Zworykin, John L. Bair and Philo J. Farnsworth.

> Commas are used to set off words in apposition.
> The Louvre, a large museum, is in France.

1. Two brothers, Orville and Wilbur Wright, invented the airplane.
2. Eli Whitney, the inventor of the cotton gin, attended Yale University.
3. The radio was invented by Marconi, an Italian.
4. Robert Fulton, the inventor of the steamboat, was an American.
5. Thomas Edison, the inventor of the light bulb, also developed the movie projector.
6. Walter Hunt invented a tiny device, the safety pin.
7. A Frenchman, Francois Blanchard, invented the parachute.
8. Samuel Morse, an American, is responsible for the telegraph.
9. An important weather gauge, the barometer, was invented in 1643.
10. W.H. Carothers developed nylon, a lightweight material.

Answer Key

Page 29

Direct Object　　　Name _____

> A noun can be used as the object word in a sentence. The word which answers the question "whom" or "what" after the verb is the Direct Object.

Circle the Direct Object in each sentence.

1. People like frozen (desserts).
2. Marco Polo brought (recipes) home from the Far East.
3. Many ices contain fruit (juices).
4. Dolly Madison served (ice cream) at a party in the 1800's.
5. Americans choose (ice cream) as their favorite dessert.
6. Americans eat three billion (quarts) a year.
7. People make (ice cream) from milk and cream.
8. Sugar, fruit and nuts give (flavor) to ice cream.
9. Egg and gelatin make the (ice cream) smooth.
10. People may choose different (flavors) of ice cream.
11. Most people choose (vanilla).
12. One big chain of restaurants advertises 40 different (flavors) of ice cream.
13. Today, large ice cream plants produce this (product).
14. Big milk trucks bring the (milk) and (cream) to the plants.
15. Other trucks bring the different (ingredients) to be used in the ice cream.
16. Often people eat (ice cream) as a dessert for meals.
17. People make (ice cream) into milkshakes.
18. Some ingredients make fancy (desserts) like parfaits.
19. We would miss this (treat) if we didn't have it.
20. Do you like (ice cream)?

Page 30

Nouns Used as Direct Objects　　　Name _____

> A noun which acts as the direct object of a verb is in the objective case. The word which answers the question "whom" or "what" after the verb is the direct object.

Underline the verb and circle the direct object in each sentence below.
The boy <u>put</u> the (skates) on the shelf.

1. The people of the United States <u>own</u> the (White House).
2. Many tourists <u>visit</u> this (home) each year.
3. James Hoban <u>designed</u> the (plans).
4. Gray sandstone <u>forms</u> the (walls).
5. The building <u>was called</u> the (President's Palace).
6. The wife of President Adams <u>hung</u> her (washing) in a room that later became the East Room.
7. Fire <u>damaged</u> the (structure) during the War of 1812.
8. White paint <u>hid</u> the (stains) from the smoke.
9. Later presidents <u>added</u> more (rooms) to the White House.
10. President Harry Truman <u>ordered</u> (repairs) for the house.
11. A steel framework now <u>supports</u> the (walls).
12. Steel also <u>strengthens</u> the (roof).
13. The whole interior <u>needed</u> (improvements).
14. Workers <u>built</u> (offices) for the president and his helpers.
15. The president <u>uses</u> the (building) as a home and a workplace.
16. The president <u>greets</u> (guests) in the Blue Room.
17. Blue silk <u>covers</u> the (walls) in the Blue Room.
18. The State Dining Room <u>holds</u> many (people).
19. Americans <u>admire</u> the (beauty) of the White House.
20. Visitors <u>respect</u> this (symbol) of our nation.

Page 31

Possessive Nouns　　　Name _____

> A noun that expresses possession or ownership is in the possessive case.
> To form the singular possessive, add 's to the singular noun.
> To form the plural possessive of nouns ending in s, add only an apostrophe. If the plural does not end in s, add 's.

Write the singular possessive, the plural and the plural possessive forms of the following nouns.

Singular	Singular Possessive	Plural	Plural Possessive
boy	boy's	boys	boys'
1. student	student's	students	students'
2. child	child's	children	children's
3. neighbor	neighbor's	neighbors	neighbors'
4. baby	baby's	babies	babies'
5. writer	writer's	writers	writers'
6. uncle	uncle's	uncles	uncles'
7. mouse	mouse's	mice	mice's
8. lady	lady's	ladies	ladies'
9. man	man's	men	men's
10. leaf	leaf's	leaves	leaves'

Underline the nouns in the possessive case.
<u>Marina's</u> book is on the desk.

1. Henry Wadsworth Longfellow is one of <u>America's</u> famous writers.
2. <u>Longfellow's</u> poems have been enjoyed by many people.
3. His two sons and three daughters are mentioned in "The <u>Children's</u> Hour".
4. Another of Longfellow's poems is "Paul <u>Revere's</u> Ride".
5. "Evangeline" is the story of one <u>woman's</u> courage.

Rewrite each phrase so that there is a noun in the possessive case.
the song of the bird — the bird's song

1. the mane of the lion — the lion's mane
2. the votes of the citizens — the citizens' votes
3. the words of the speaker — the speaker's words
4. the home of my grandparents — my grandparents' home
5. the dresses of the women — the women's dresses

Page 32

Possessives　　　Name _____

> A noun that expresses possession or ownership is in the possessive case.
> To form the singular possessive, add 's to the nominative singular of the noun.
> To form the plural possessive of nouns ending in s, add only an apostrophe. If the nominative plural does not end in s, add 's.

Write the singular possessive, the plural and the plural possessive forms.

Singular	Singular Possessive	Plural	Plural Possessive
1. teacher	teacher's	teachers	teachers'
2. baby	baby's	babies	babies'
3. child	child's	children	children's
4. woman	woman's	women	women's
5. team	team's	teams	teams'
6. friend	friend's	friends	friends'
7. man	man's	men	men's
8. dog	dog's	dogs	dogs'
9. girl	girl's	girls	girls'
10. doctor	doctor's	doctors	doctors'

Underline the possessive form of the noun in each sentence.

1. Booker T. Washington is one of <u>America's</u> famous black men.
2. <u>Washington's</u> book Up From Slavery tells the story of his life.
3. He became the <u>slaves'</u> spokesman.
4. Washington traveled around the world telling of the <u>Negroes'</u> problems.
5. <u>Washington's</u> formal education was at Hampton Institute for Negroes.
6. <u>Booker's</u> grades were very high.
7. He became one of the <u>school's</u> leading teachers.
8. He founded a <u>Negroes'</u> school in 1881 in Tuskegee, Alabama.
9. The first classes were held in a <u>church's</u> meeting room.
10. The <u>school's</u> name became Tuskegee Institute.

Answer Key

Page 33

Nouns Used as Objects of Prepositions

Name _____

A noun used as the object of a preposition is in the objective case. The word that answers the question "whom" or "what" after the preposition is the object of that preposition.

In the following sentences, underline the preposition and circle its object.
The jet roared <u>across</u> the (sky)

1. Weather is often a topic <u>for</u> (discussion)
2. Rain and snow are a part <u>of</u> the (weather)
3. Clouds, heat waves and periods <u>of</u> (cold) also affect the weather.
4. People must prepare <u>for</u> quick (changes) <u>in</u> the (weather)
5. Not everyone wants the same kind <u>of</u> (weather)
6. A farmer may hope <u>for</u> (rain)
7. His neighbor might want sunny weather <u>for</u> a (picnic)
8. Some people may wish <u>for</u> a heavy (snowstorm) <u>for</u> (skiing)
9. Not everyone likes warm weather <u>in</u> early (spring)
10. They know snow <u>in</u> the (mountains) may melt too quickly.
11. This could result <u>in</u> (floods)
12. Weather is an important factor <u>in</u> a person's (life)
13. Bad weather may ruin crops and raise the cost <u>of</u> (food)
14. It may cause forest fires or kill livestock <u>on</u> the (range)
15. The weather affects our lives in many (ways)
16. In the summer, people complain <u>about</u> the (humidity)
17. Humidity is the amount <u>of</u> moisture <u>in</u> the (air)
18. A warm day seems hotter <u>with</u> higher (humidity)
19. <u>Inside</u> our (home) we can control certain factors.
20. We have learned much <u>from</u> scientific (experiments)

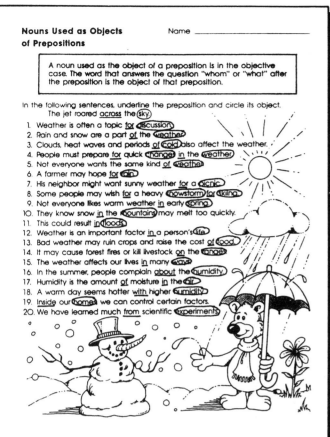

Page 33

Page 34

Nouns Used as Indirect Objects

Name _____

A noun which acts as an indirect object is in the objective case. The indirect object indicates to whom or for whom the action is performed.

Underline the direct object and circle the indirect object.
The teacher gave (Susan) the <u>book</u>.

1. Thomas Edison gave the (world) many useful <u>inventions</u>.
2. He gave (man) a better <u>means</u> of lighting.
3. Candles gave (people) <u>light</u> in earlier times.
4. Kerosene gave (lamps) the necessary <u>fuel</u> to burn.
5. Edison paid his (assistants) <u>money</u> to research better lighting.
6. These helpers offered (Edison) <u>information</u> they found.
7. Edison gave (people) the electric light <u>bulb</u>.
8. Edison offered (mankind) many other <u>ideas</u> to save time and energy.
9. His experiments provided (men) an easier <u>way</u> of life.
10. We owe (Thomas Edison) our <u>gratitude</u>.

Appositive in the Objective Case

A noun in apposition with a direct object, indirect object or object of a preposition is in the objective case.

Circle the noun in apposition and underline the word it explains.
We need the <u>device</u>, the (telephone)

1. An important <u>device</u> was discovered by the famous <u>inventor</u>, (Alexander Graham Bell)
2. Alexander G. Bell invented a modern-day <u>tool</u>, the (telephone)
3. Bell was born in a foreign <u>country</u>, (Scotland)
4. At night, he worked on his favorite <u>hobby</u>, (electricity)
5. Bell had an <u>assistant</u>, (Thomas Watson)
6. Watson built an <u>instrument</u>, the harmonic (telegraph) for Bell.
7. Together, they worked on this <u>project</u>, the (telephone)
8. Watson heard <u>sounds</u>, the first (words) over the telephone.
9. Years later, Bell talked to Watson across lines in another <u>city</u>, (San Francisco)
10. Alexander Graham Bell will be remembered as a great <u>man</u>, the (inventor) of the telephone.

Page 34

Page 35

Recognition of Verbs

Name _____

A verb is a word that expresses action or being.

Circle the verb in each sentence. Tell if it is an action A verb or a being B verb.

A 1. Many people (play) summer sports.
B 2. However, there (are) many winter sports.
B 3. Skiing and skating (are) popular.
B 4. Skating (is) an old sport.
A 5. Some skaters (work) for faster speeds.
A 6. Other skaters (like) figure skating better.
B 7. Figure skating (is) fancy skating.
A 8. Many people (enjoy) ice hockey.
B 9. Skating (is) an important part of this sport.
A 10. Players (shoot) a puck into a goal net.
A 11. Boys and girls (coast) down snowy hills on sleds.
B 12. Toboggans (are) fun, too.
B 13. Skiing (is) another favorite winter sport.
A 14. Skiing down slopes (takes) great skill.
A 15. Ski jumpers (leap) high into the air.
A 16. They (sail) gracefully through the air.
B 17. The landing (is) tricky.
A 18. Contestants (participate) in the Winter Olympics.
A 19. These games (happen) every four years.
A 20. People (watch) the Olympics with much interest.

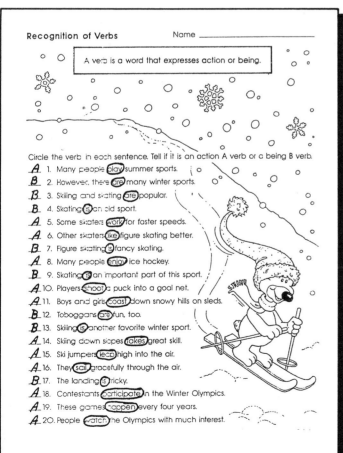

Page 35

Page 36

Action and Being Verbs

Name _____

A verb is a word which expresses action or being. The verb is the most important word in a sentence. There can be no sentence without the verb.

Write S on the line before each group of words which is a sentence and underline the verb in each. Write N on the line before each group of words that is not a sentence.

N Across the bridge. S We walked across the bridge.

S 1. Paul Revere <u>was</u> a patriotic American.
N 2. The ride of Paul Revere
S 3. Revere <u>lived</u> in Boston during the time of the American Revolution.
S 4. He <u>belonged</u> to a group of patriots.
N 5. Part of the Boston Tea Party
N 6. The British troops in Boston
S 7. The tea party <u>was</u> a warning to England
S 8. The colonists <u>wanted</u> some say in their own government
N 9. Orders of the English king.
S 10. The colonists <u>fought</u> for their freedom

Underline the verb in each sentence and tell whether it is an action verb or a being verb.

action The wolf <u>howled</u> in the distance. being A wolf is an animal.

a 1. The colonists <u>stored</u> ammunition at Concord, near Boston.
b 2. The minutemen <u>were</u> American soldiers ready for battle.
b 3. The British army <u>was</u> on the march.
a 4. They <u>wanted</u> the ammunition at Concord.
b 5. Paul Revere <u>was</u> the messenger of the patriots.
a 6. He <u>watched</u> for the signal from Old North Church in Boston.
a 7. Two lanterns <u>flashed</u> in the church tower.
a 8. He <u>raced</u> to the minutemen.
a 9. The British <u>came</u> by water.
a 10. Paul Revere <u>warned</u> the American soldiers in time.

Page 36

Answer Key

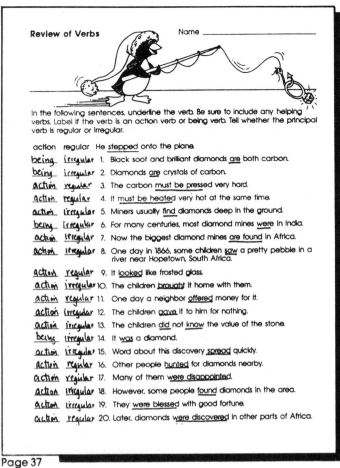

Review of Verbs

Name _____

In the following sentences, underline the verb. Be sure to include any helping verbs. Label if the verb is an action verb or being verb. Tell whether the principal verb is regular or irregular.

action regular He stepped onto the plane.

being	irregular	1. Black soot and brilliant diamonds are both carbon.
being	irregular	2. Diamonds are crystals of carbon.
action	regular	3. The carbon must be pressed very hard.
action	regular	4. It must be heated very hot at the same time.
action	irregular	5. Miners usually find diamonds deep in the ground.
being	irregular	6. For many centuries, most diamond mines were in India.
action	irregular	7. Now the biggest diamond mines are found in Africa.
action	irregular	8. One day in 1866, some children saw a pretty pebble in a river near Hopetown, South Africa.
action	regular	9. It looked like frosted glass.
action	irregular	10. The children brought it home with them.
action	regular	11. One day a neighbor offered money for it.
action	irregular	12. The children gave it to him for nothing.
action	irregular	13. The children did not know the value of the stone.
being	irregular	14. It was a diamond.
action	irregular	15. Word about this discovery spread quickly.
action	regular	16. Other people hunted for diamonds nearby.
action	regular	17. Many of them were disappointed.
action	irregular	18. However, some people found diamonds in the area.
action	irregular	19. They were blessed with good fortune.
action	regular	20. Later, diamonds were discovered in other parts of Africa.

Page 37

Verb Phrases

Name _____

A group of words that do the job of a single verb is called a verb phrase. In a verb phrase, there is one principal verb and one or more helping verbs.

Circle the verb phrase in each sentence.
These sentences (were written) about Rudyard Kipling.

1. Rudyard Kipling (was born) in Bombay, India.
2. His English father (was teaching) art in India.
3. Kipling (had heard) jungle stories from the native people.
4. The Indian people (had told) these stories to their own children.
5. At the age of six, Rudyard (was sent) to school in England.
6. However, he (could) not (attend) school.
7. He (had become) very ill.
8. Kipling (could) not (go) to school for 5 years.
9. After many years, he (had completed) his basic education.
10. At this time, Kipling's father (was working) in Lahore, India.
11. Rudyard (would return) to that country.
12. His job in India (would be writing) for a newspaper.
13. He (had written) several poems and short stories for the newspaper.
14. Later, these poems and stories (were published) in two books.
15. He (had become) famous by the age of 26.
16. One of his most famous books (was written) for his children.
17. That book (is called) The Jungle Book.
18. Captains Courageous (was written) during his years in Vermont.
19. After a few years in America, Kipling (had planned) a return to England.
20. Rudyard Kipling (is loved) around the world for his children's stories.

Page 38

Verb Phrases

Name _____

A group of words that does the job of a single verb is called a verb phrase. In a verb phrase, there is one principal verb and one or more helping or auxiliary verbs.

Circle the verb phrases in the following sentences.
The tourists (had lost) their way.

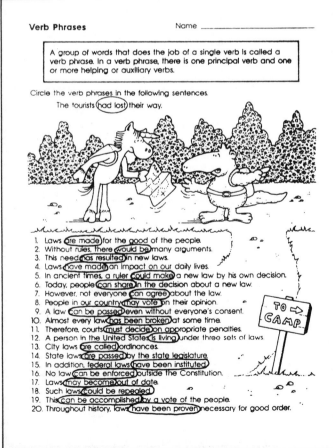

1. Laws (are made) for the good of the people.
2. Without rules, there (would be) many arguments.
3. This need (has resulted) in new laws.
4. Laws (have made) an impact on our daily lives.
5. In ancient times, a ruler (could make) a new law by his own decision.
6. Today, people (can share) in the decision about a new law.
7. However, not everyone (can agree) about the law.
8. People in our country (may vote) on their opinion.
9. A law (can be passed) even without everyone's consent.
10. Almost every law (has been broken) at some time.
11. Therefore, courts (must decide) on appropriate penalties.
12. A person in the United States (is living) under three sets of laws.
13. City laws (are called) ordinances.
14. State laws (are passed) by the state legislature.
15. In addition, federal laws (have been instituted).
16. No law (can be enforced) outside the Constitution.
17. Laws (may become) out of date.
18. Such laws (could be repealed).
19. This (can be accomplished) by a vote of the people.
20. Throughout history, laws (have been proven) necessary for good order.

Page 39

Regular Verbs

Name _____

The principal parts of a verb are the present, past and past participle. A regular verb forms its past and past participle by adding -d or -ed to the present. The past participle always uses a helping verb with the main verb.

Write the past and past participle forms of the following verbs.

Present	Past	Past Participle (Always used with a helping verb)
bake	baked	baked
1. finish	finished	finished
2. call	called	called
3. open	opened	opened
4. delay	delayed	delayed
5. follow	followed	followed
6. gather	gathered	gathered
7. talk	talked	stumbled
8. stumble	stumbled	helped
9. help	helped	whispered
10. whisper	whispered	

Label the forms of the verbs.
like present
peeked past
had scrambled past participle

1. explored — past
2. wait — present
3. skated — past
4. have hurried — past participle
5. pick — present
6. had leaped — past participle
7. raced — past
8. has trimmed — past participle
9. sprinkle — present
10. had invented — past participle

has blown   blown
blow   blow

Page 40

Answer Key

Page 41

Regular Verbs   Name _____

> The principal parts of a verb are the present, past and past participle. A regular verb is one that forms its past and past participle by adding -d or -ed to the present. The past participle always uses a helping or auxiliary verb with the main verb.

Write the past and past participle forms of the following verbs.

Present	Past	Past Participle (used with auxiliary)
plan	planned	planned
hope	hoped	hoped
1. reach	reached	had reached
2. climb	climbed	has climbed
3. offer	offered	had offered
4. cooperate	cooperated	had cooperated
5. believe	believed	has believed
6. walk	walked	has walked
7. notice	noticed	had noticed
8. move	moved	had moved
9. appear	appeared	had appeared
10. float	floated	had floated
11. study	studied	had studied
12. paint	painted	has painted
13. clean	cleaned	has painted
14. visit	visited	have visited
15. call	called	have called

Label the forms of the verbs below.

stop	—	present
placed	—	past
has played	—	past participle

1. arranged — past
2. has delivered — past participle
3. watch — present
4. had assigned — past participle
5. pour — present
6. danced — past
7. scramble — present
8. have purchased — past participle
9. changed — past
10. suggest — present
11. covered — past
12. has listened — past participle
13. plunge — present
14. tested — past

Page 42

Irregular Verbs   Name _____

> An irregular verb is one that does not form its past and past participle by adding -d or -ed to its present. The past participle form always uses a helping or auxiliary verb.

Write the past and past participle forms of these irregular verbs.

Present	Past	Past Participle (used with auxiliary)
do	did	done
see	saw	seen
go	went	gone
bring	brought	brought
fall	fell	fallen
run	ran	run
make	made	made
forget	forgot	forgotten
give	gave	given
have	had	had
write	wrote	written
meet	met	met
know	knew	known
speak	spoke	spoken
win	won	won
stand	stood	stood
take	took	taken
sit	sat	sat
grow	grew	grown
choose	chose	chosen
burst	burst	burst
freeze	froze	frozen

Page 43

Drill on Irregular Verbs   Name _____

> The following sentences have irregular verbs. Underline the verb in each sentence. Label the principal verb according to its present, past or past participle form.

past participle — Lighthouses have sent signals to ships.

present 1. Far out at sea, ships run into few dangers.
present 2. A bad storm makes a trip rough.
present 3. Many stories about sailing tell of shipwrecks on rocky coasts.
past participle 4. Many ships have sunk near dangerous reefs.
past participle 5. For hundreds of years, men have built lighthouses.
past participle 6. Lighthouses often have kept ships out of danger.
past participle 7. Their lights have shown faithfully through the years.
past 8. The earliest lighthouses had bonfires for light.
past 9. In time, candles took the place of bonfires.
past 10. Later, oil lamps came into use.
past 11. Then, electric lamps brought a convenient means of light.
present 12. Today, most lighthouses have electric lamps with lenses and reflectors.
past participle 13. Rocky islands have become the usual location for lighthouses.
past 14. Lighthouse keepers often led lonely lives.
present 15. Now most lights in lighthouses run automatically.
present 16. This gives the lighthouse keepers more free time.
present 17. However, bad weather still gives lighthouse keepers much work.
present 18. They send out radio signals to the ships.
past participle 19. The sound of the foghorn has kept many ships out of danger.
present 20. All around the world, sailors know the importance of lighthouses and their keepers.

Page 44

Drill on Irregular Verbs   Name _____

> In each of the following sentences, fill in the form of the irregular verb that is indicated.

I saw the parade.

1. George Washington chose the location for the capital of the United States. (Past of choose)
2. He had chosen a site on the Potomac River. (Past participle of choose)
3. People have written the letters "DC" after the name of this city. (Past participle of write)
4. The letters stand for the "District of Columbia". (Present of stand)
5. The new government had taken land from Virginia and Maryland as the site of the city. (Past participle of take)
6. Officials had given the job of city planner to Major L'Enfant. (Past participle of give)
7. Major L'Enfant had laid out an interesting pattern for the streets. (Past participle of lay)
8. Many of them go out like spokes on a wheel. (Present of go)
9. Fine parks and buildings make the city extremely beautiful. (Present of make)
10. The government has built many of the buildings. (Past participle of build)
11. Washington became the official capital of the United States in 1800. (Past of become)
12. During the War of 1812, the city fell into the hands of the British. (Past of fall)
13. The work of the national government has grown. (Past participle of grow)
14. New buildings have been built from time to time. (Past participle of build)
15. Monuments rise above other buildings. (Present of rise)
16. Pennsylvania Avenue has become the most famous street in Washington, DC. (Past participle of become)
17. Many great parades have gone down this avenue. (Past participle of go)
18. People have ridden for hours to see this great city. (Past participle of ride)
19. No one forgets the beauty of Washington, DC. (Present of forget)
20. Many people have spent their vacations in this city. (Past participle of spend)

Answer Key

Page 45

Drill on Irregular Verbs Name _____

In each of the following sentences, fill in the form of the irregular verb that is indicated.

We <u>bought</u> a basket of apples. (past of buy)

1. Many of us have __seen__ pictures of the Pilgrims. (past participle of see)
2. We __knew__ a little about their adventures. (present of know)
3. The Pilgrims __left__ England on September 17, 1620. (past of leave)
4. One hundred and two people __fled__ England in search of freedom. (past of flee)
5. They __came__ to America on the "Mayflower". (past of come)
6. They had __brought__ few belongings with them. (past participle of bring)
7. The voyage __took__ two months and five days. (past of take)
8. The Pilgrims __made__ an agreement about just laws. (past of make)
9. It was __known__ as the Mayflower Compact. (past participle of know)
10. The Pilgrims __set__ up their new homes. (past of set)
11. This __began__ the colony of Plymouth. (past of begin)
12. The Pilgrims __had chosen__ to leave England for an important reason. (past participle of choose)
13. Freedom of worship __meant__ a great deal to them. (past of mean)
14. They __saw__ America as a new beginning. (past of see)
15. They __found__ many hardships in this new land. (past of find)
16. The Pilgrims never __forgot__ their problems in England. (past of forget)
17. This __kept__ them strong in their efforts. (past of keep)
18. They __fought__ hard against disease and starvation. (past of fight)
19. In the spring, the Mayflower __set__ out for a return trip to England. (past of set)
20. The Pilgrims must have __felt__ homesick with the ship's departure. (past participle of feel)

Page 46

Linking Verbs Name _____

A linking verb couples or links a noun, pronoun or adjective to the subject in the sentence. The verb "be" and its various forms is the most common linking verb.

Underline the linking verb and circle the two words joined by that verb.

(London) is the (capital) of England.

1. A (silkworm) is a (caterpillar) of the silkworm moth.
2. (Silk) is a (material) from the silkworm.
3. (This) is a smooth (material).
4. The (texture) of the fabric is (soft).
5. (China) is (famous) for its silk.
6. (Silk-making) is a complicated (process).
7. Mulberry (leaves) are the (diet) of silkworms.
8. Healthy mulberry (trees) are (important) to the silk industry.
9. (Silkworms) are adult (spinners) 25 days after hatching.
10. About (one-fifth) of their weight is (silk).
11. (Silk) is a (thread) from the silkworm's body.
12. (Silk) is the (substance) of the silkworm's cocoon.
13. The (silk) of a cocoon is one long unbroken (thread).
14. The (joining) of the threads of several cocoons is a (skill).
15. A (skein) is a (coil) of the silken threads.
16. For hundreds of years, (silk) was a (luxury).
17. (Silk) was the most beautiful (material) for clothing.
18. Even today (silk) is an important (fabric).
19. (It) is a favorite (fabric) among many women.
20. Luxurious (silks) are sometimes (multi-colored).

Page 47

Linking Verbs Name _____

A linking verb couples or links a noun, pronoun or adjective to the subject in the sentence. The verb **be** and its various forms is the most common linking verb.

Underline the linking verb and circle the two words joined by that verb.

The (capital) of the United States is (Washington, D.C.)

1. (Four) of the first five presidents were (men) from the state of Virginia.
2. (Thomas Jefferson) was (one) of them.
3. (Monticello) was the (home) of his home.
4. (It) is still a favorite tourist (attraction) in Virginia.
5. (He) was the third (president) of the United States.
6. (He) was (famous) early in our country's history.
7. (Jefferson) was a true (patriot).
8. (He) was the (author) of the Declaration of Independence.
9. (Thomas Jefferson) was (president) from 1801 to 1809.
10. The (United States) was a small (country) during Jefferson's term in office.
11. A very large (area) of land was a (purchase) from France.
12. The (area) was (land) west of the Mississippi River.
13. (It) was (land) for new states.
14. (Thomas Jefferson) was (famous) for the purchase of the Louisiana Territory.
15. The (Louisiana Purchase) was (important) for the growth of our country.
16. (Science) and (music) were (interests) of Thomas Jefferson.
17. (He) was also a good (architect).
18. Another (interest) of his was (education).
19. (He) was the (founder) of the University of Virginia.
20. (Thomas Jefferson) was a really great (American).

Page 48

Transitive Verbs Name _____

A transitive verb shows action passing from a doer to a receiver. A verb is transitive if it has a direct object or if it contains a form of the verb be plus a past participle.

Underline each transitive verb and circle the receiver of the action.

The workers <u>completed</u> the (job)

1. Locks and keys <u>mean</u> (safety) for people and their possessions.
2. Even the ancient Egyptions <u>used</u> (locks).
3. Almost all locks <u>have</u> (keys).
4. However, a combination lock <u>has</u> no (key).
5. A person <u>uses</u> a (combination) of numbers for this type of lock.
6. Every lock <u>has</u> a (bolt).
7. A key or knob <u>moves</u> the (bolt).
8. Linus Yale <u>invented</u> the Yale (lock) in 1848.
9. The Yale lock <u>needs</u> a (key).
10. The key <u>moves</u> little (pins) in the lock.
11. This <u>frees</u> the (bolt).
12. Bank vaults <u>have</u> large combination (locks).
13. The banker <u>turns</u> the (knob) on the combination lock to just the right numbers.
14. Only a few employees of the bank <u>will know</u> the (combination).
15. Some vaults <u>have</u> time (locks).
16. Clockworks in the lock <u>make</u> this (setting) possible.
17. Today almost every grown person <u>carries</u> several (keys).
18. Keys <u>open</u> (locks) to houses and cars.
19. Some cars <u>need</u> two (keys) for operation.
20. This common use of locks <u>protects</u> (property).

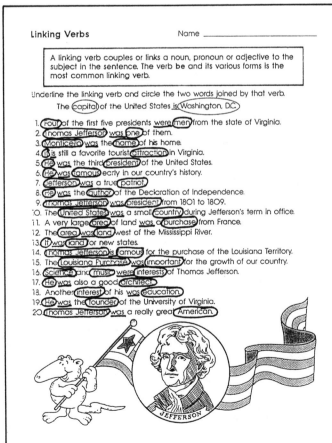

Page 49

Transitive Verbs   Name _____

| A transitive verb shows action passing from a doer to a receiver. |

Underline each transitive verb and circle the receiver of the action.

Clarise <u>read</u> the (newspaper)

1. Most people <u>like</u> (plants)
2. They <u>enjoy</u> (plants) even in the winter.
3. Many people <u>grow</u> (plants) all year long.
4. Both men and women <u>raise</u> (flowers)
5. Flower shops <u>sell</u> many potted (plants)
6. Florists <u>tell</u> (purchasers) about proper care.
7. Proper sunlight <u>helps</u> (plants)
8. Some plants <u>require</u> (water) every day.
9. Others <u>need</u> special plant (food)
10. Some plants <u>form</u> beautiful (leaves)
11. Certain plants <u>produce</u> (blooms)
12. A grapefruit seed <u>becomes</u> a pretty (plant)
13. Growers <u>raise</u> new (violets) from the old leaves.
14. People <u>use</u> small (branches) for new plants.
15. Many people <u>grow</u> (plants) as a hobby.
16. Many individuals <u>keep</u> (plants) in their homes.
17. Some people <u>use</u> (greenhouses) for indoor gardens.
18. Small indoor greenhouses <u>are called</u> (terrariums)
19. I <u>have</u> several (plants) in my home.
20. My garden <u>contains</u> many (flowers) in the spring and summer.

Page 50

Intransitive Verbs   Name _____

| An intransitive verb is one that has no receiver of its action. The subject is the doer of the action. |

Underline the intransitive verb and circle the doer of the action.

Some (flowers) <u>grow</u> very well.

1. Many (kinds) of flowers <u>grow</u> in our gardens.
2. Some garden (plants) <u>grow</u> tall.
3. (Many) of the plants <u>stand</u> straight all by themselves.
4. (Vines) <u>climb</u> along fences or poles.
5. Some garden (flowers) <u>live</u> longer than others.
6. Some (flowers) <u>live</u> for two seasons.
7. A long growing (season) <u>is needed</u> for some flowers.
8. (They) <u>must be planted</u> early in the spring.
9. Some (plants) <u>are raised</u> indoors for a time.
10. Then (they) <u>can be transplanted</u> outdoors.
11. Often (petunias) <u>are started</u> indoors.
12. Some (flowers) <u>grow</u> from seeds.
13. Many garden (flowers) <u>are raised</u> from bulbs.
14. (Tulips) <u>grow</u> from bulbs.
15. Certain (types) of soil <u>are required</u> for some plants.
16. Very rich (soil) is needed for sweet peas.
17. (Zinnias) <u>will grow</u> in poor soil.
18. However, (they) <u>do not grow</u> well in shade.
19. Today (flowers) <u>are being improved</u>.
20. (Growers) <u>are working</u> for better varieties of garden flowers.

Page 51

Intransitive Verbs   Name _____

| An intransitive verb is one which has no receiver of its action. The subject is the doer of the action. |

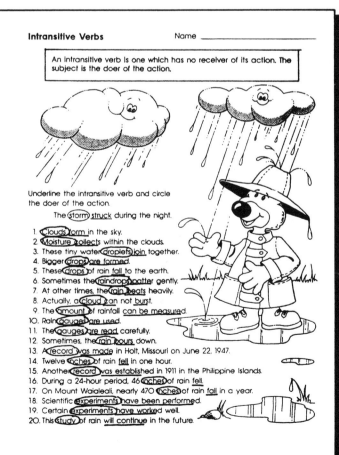

Underline the intransitive verb and circle the doer of the action.

The (storm) <u>struck</u> during the night.

1. (Clouds) <u>form</u> in the sky.
2. (Moisture) <u>collects</u> within the clouds.
3. These tiny water (droplets) <u>join</u> together.
4. Bigger (drops) <u>are formed</u>.
5. These (drops) of rain <u>fall</u> to the earth.
6. Sometimes the (raindrops) <u>patter</u> gently.
7. At other times, the (rain) <u>beats</u> heavily.
8. Actually, a (cloud) <u>can not burst</u>.
9. The (amount) of rainfall <u>can be measured</u>.
10. Rain (gauges) <u>are used</u>.
11. The (gauges) <u>are read</u> carefully.
12. Sometimes, the (rain) <u>pours</u> down.
13. A (record) <u>was made</u> in Holt, Missouri on June 22, 1947.
14. Twelve (inches) of rain <u>fell</u> in one hour.
15. Another (record) <u>was established</u> in 1911 in the Philippine Islands.
16. During a 24-hour period, 46 (inches) of rain fell.
17. On Mount Waialeali, nearly 470 (inches) of rain <u>fall</u> in a year.
18. Scientific (experiments) <u>have been performed</u>.
19. Certain (experiments) <u>have worked</u> well.
20. This (study) of rain <u>will continue</u> in the future.

Page 52

Simple Tense   Name _____

| Tense indicates the time of the action or being. There are three simple tenses: present, past and future.

Present tense indicates action or being in present time.
Past tense indicates action or being in past time.
Future tense indicates action or being in future time.
The auxiliary verbs **will** and **shall** are used with the principal verb to form the future tense. |

Underline the verb and tell whether it is in the present, past or future tense.

Present   Jane <u>writes</u> poetry.
Past   Jane <u>wrote</u> a poem.
Future   Jane <u>will write</u> a poem for English class.

present 1. Some people <u>call</u> glaciers great sheets of ice.
present 2. Others <u>refer</u> to them as giant rivers of ice.
future 3. In the far north and south, glaciers <u>will stretch</u> to the sea.
present 4. Sometimes the ice <u>pushes</u> past the edge of the land.
present 5. Huge pieces of ice <u>break</u> from the glaciers.
past 6. Scientists <u>named</u> these floating glaciers icebergs.
past 7. One explorer <u>compared</u> the size of a southern iceberg to a 50-story building.
past 8. Another scientist <u>measured</u> a northern iceberg as more than 100 feet tall.
present 9. Many northern icebergs <u>come</u> from the icecap of Greenland.
present 10. Some icebergs <u>float</u> into warmer waters.
future 11. An iceberg <u>will travel</u> as far as 2000 miles.
future 12. All the colors of the rainbow <u>will appear</u> in an iceberg in the sunlight.
future 13. Ocean waves <u>will cut</u> caves in some icebergs.
past 14. In the past, icebergs <u>presented</u> problems to ships.
past 15. Researchers <u>discovered</u> the largest parts of icebergs below the surface of the water.
present 16. This hidden part <u>spreads</u> into a great shelf of ice.
past 17. An iceberg <u>was</u> the cause of the greatest shipwreck in this century.
past 18. An iceberg in the North Atlantic <u>caused</u> the destruction of the "Titanic".

Answer Key

Tense   Name _____

> Tense indicates the time of the action or being. There are three simple tenses: present, past and future.
>   Present tense indicates action or being in present time.
>   Past tense indicates action or being in past time.
>   Future tense indicates action or being in future time. The auxiliary verbs **will** and **shall** are used with the principal verb to form the future tense.

Underline the verb and tell whether it is in the present tense, past tense or future tense.

   PRESENT   They <u>complete</u> their work.
   PAST   They <u>completed</u> their work.
   FUTURE   They <u>will complete</u> their work.

present 1. Scientists <u>use</u> microscopes to study tiny things.
present 2. A microscope <u>enlarges</u> things many times their normal size.
future 3. For example, particles of clay <u>will look</u> larger than usual.
future 4. Red cells from a person's blood <u>will appear</u> clearer in size and shape.
past 5. The word "microscope" <u>came</u> from the Greeks.
future 6. Many microscopes <u>will have</u> only one lens each.
future 7. Some microscopes <u>will have</u> more than one lens.
past 8. We <u>called</u> this type a compound microscope.
present 9. The lenses <u>increase</u> the appearance of objects.
past 10. The inventor of the microscope <u>was</u> probably a Dutch spectacle maker.
present 11. We <u>know</u> him as Zacharias Janssen.
past 12. He <u>gave</u> the Archduke of Austria a compound microscope in 1590.
past 13. Some doctors <u>discovered</u> important medical facts with a microscope.
past 14. Anton van Leeuwenhoek <u>was</u> a scientist in Holland 300 years ago.
past 15. He <u>observed</u> bacteria with a microscope.
past 16. He <u>realized</u> the importance of the microscope.
present 17. Today there <u>are</u> other kinds of microscopes.
past 18. Scientists <u>discovered</u> the planet, Pluto, with the Blink microscope.

Page 53

Imperative Mood   Name _____

> The imperative mood is used to express a command in the second person. In the imperative mood, the subject of the sentence is always you, either singular or plural. The subject word is rarely expressed.

Fill in the blanks with a verb in the imperative mood.

   <u>Cut</u> the grass.   *Answers will vary.*

1. _____ the assignment carefully.
2. _____ the door quietly.
3. Always _____ distinctly.
4. _____ the table.
5. _____ the packages into the house.
6. _____ the seeds in the garden.
7. _____ the piano every day.
8. _____ the tickets for the concert.
9. Children, _____ your notes for the test.
10. _____ the doorbell.
11. _____ a good sport in all competitions.
12. _____ to the store for me, please.
13. _____ the flag in the morning.
14. Always _____ only the truth.
15. _____ your best manners.
16. _____ your name on the check.
17. _____ your bedroom on Saturday.
18. _____ the directions at the top of the page.
19. _____ the letters at the post office.
20. _____ the police in case of an emergency.

Page 54

Agreement of Verb With Subject   Name _____

> A singular subject needs a singular verb. A plural subject needs a plural verb. In most cases, the verb does not require a change in form to agree with its subject. However, in the third person of the present tense, the singular verb ends in **s**.
>   My friend **lives** near.
>   My friends **live** near.

Circle the correct verb form in each sentence below.

1. Erosion (**is**, are) the wearing away of land.
2. Wind, waves, ice and running water (does, **do**) most of the wearing away of land.
3. Wind-blown sand sometimes (**carves**, carve) rocks into strange shapes.
4. Waves also (wears, **wear**) away solid rock.
5. Rivers of ice (acts, **act**) like plows.
6. They (**push**, pushes) rocks and soil ahead of them.
7. These glaciers (gouges, **gouge**) deep valleys in the land.
8. Running water (**is**, are) the chief element in erosion.
9. Rainwater (**does**, do) more erosive damage than wind, waves and ice all together.
10. Loose soil (**wears**, wear) away faster than solid rock.
11. The Mississippi River (**dumps**, dump) tons of soil into the Gulf of Mexico each year.
12. Farmers (understands, **understand**) that erosion is the greatest enemy of their soil.
13. Erosion (**occurs**, occur) faster on soil without plant coverings.
14. A gully in a field (**is**, are) a danger sign.
15. Plant roots (helps, **help**) hold the soil in place.
16. Erosion (**takes**, take) place faster on hillsides than on level ground.
17. With this information, farmers (**fight**, fights) the effects of erosion.
18. They (plows, **plow**) fields on hillsides horizontally.
19. Today, people (knows, **know**) about the problem of erosion.
20. We (works, **work**) to prevent further damage to our valuable land.

Page 55

Personal Pronouns   Name _____

> A word used in place of a noun is a pronoun. A personal pronoun indicates the speaker, the one spoken to or the one spoken of.
>   First person pronouns are: I, mine, me, we, ours and us.
>   Second person pronouns are: you and yours.
>   Third person pronouns are: he, she, it, his, hers, its, him, her, they, theirs and them.

Place the number 1 above pronouns of the first person, the number 2 above the pronouns of the second person, and the number 3 above pronouns of the third person.

   We will study a famous man.

1. Many of us have studied about Robert E. Lee.
2. We will study about him now.
3. He became a famous and respected man.
4. When Robert's father died, He was left to care for his invalid mother.
5. Whenever she was well enough, Robert took her for a drive in the country.
6. He became a West Point cadet at eighteen.
7. His family said they couldn't be prouder.
8. You can imagine the pride that was theirs.
9. He never received even one demerit at school.
10. I think that is remarkable.
11. At graduation, Lee's classmates said they admired him.
12. Whose school record is better, his or yours?
13. During the Mexican War, Lee showed us his great courage.
14. He played an important role in the Civil War.
15. It was the war between the North and South.
16. Lee loved this country of ours, but his loyalty fell with the South.
17. You can imagine how difficult it was for him to fight against the Union.
18. General Lee proved he was a great general, gaining many victories.
19. It is clear to me that General Lee was a man of honor.
20. We can respect him and the strength he showed.

Page 56

Answer Key

Page 57

Personal Pronouns   Name _____

> The pronouns which denote the person spoken to are: **you** and **yours**.

In each of the following sentences, draw a circle around the pronoun which denotes the person spoken to.

Flying will be exciting for (you).

1. Have (you) ever ridden in a airplane?
2. (You) will feel excitement when the plane takes off.
3. The first thing they tell (you) is to fasten your seat belts.
4. The flight attendant will make (your) flight comfortable.
5. This seat is (yours).
6. Would (you) like something to drink?
7. Is this baggage (yours)?
8. (You) sometimes can see towns far below.
9. Do (you) have your ticket, sir?
10. The pilot will talk to (you) over the intercom.
11. He will let (you) know if you have to fasten your seat belts.
12. (You) may be served a meal.
13. There are magazines for (you) to read.
14. Some flights show movies for (you) to enjoy.
15. This book is (yours) to keep.
16. I've liked sitting next to (you) on the plane.
17. (Yours) was the best seat by the window.
18. The pilot will let (you) know when he is ready to land.
19. When the plane lands, take what is (yours).
20. (You) will enjoy traveling by plane.

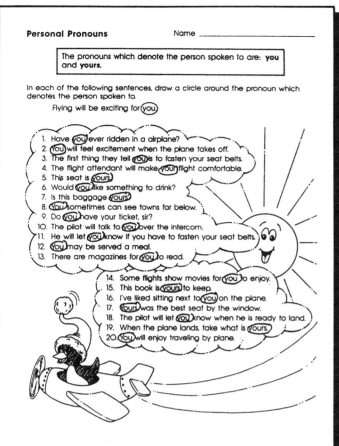

Page 58

Number and Gender of Pronouns   Name _____

> A singular pronoun replaces a singular noun. A plural pronoun replaces a plural noun.
> The singular pronouns are: I, mine, me, you, yours, he, she, it, his, hers, its and him.
> The plural pronouns are: we, ours, you, yours, they, theirs, us and them.

Underline the personal pronouns. Place an S above the singular pronouns and a P above the plural pronouns.

I(S) saw them(P) yesterday.

1. I(S) love watching a parade.
2. She(S) arrived with them(P) an hour before it(S) was to begin.
3. Can you(P) girls hear the band playing?
4. They(P) are marching down the street.
5. You(S) may stand next to me(S) for a better view.
6. Ours(P) was the best place along the parade route.
7. One man in the parade sang songs for us(P).
8. He(S) asked us(P) to sing with him(S).
9. We(P) enjoyed the clowns most of all.
10. It(S) was a long parade, and we(P) were tired when it(S) ended.

> A pronoun that indicates male sex is masculine gender. A pronoun that indicates female sex is feminine gender. A pronoun that indicates objects having no sex is neuter gender.
> The masculine pronouns are: he, his and him.
> The feminine pronouns are: she, hers and her.
> The neuter pronouns are: it and its.
> Plural pronouns may indicate all three genders.

Write a pronoun to take the place of each noun.

books – they

1. document it
2. actress she/her
3. Charles he/him
4. keys they/them
5. rabbit it
6. sisters they/them
7. boy he/him
8. television it
9. father he/him
10. tourists they/them
11. students they/them
12. computer it
13. nephew he/him
14. journey it
15. children they/them
16. waiter he/him
17. Victoria she/her
18. tulips they/them
19. program it
20. Michael he/him

Page 59

Possessive Pronouns   Name _____

> Pronouns used to indicate ownership or possession are called possessive pronouns.
> The possessive pronouns are: mine, yours, his, hers, its, ours and theirs.

Underline the possessive pronouns in the following sentences.

That book is hers.

1. The idea for this story is mine.
2. Have you thought about yours?
3. Hers is very interesting.
4. I wonder what his will be like?
5. Let's read theirs now.
6. The teacher helped me with mine.
7. Hers will not be finished until tomorrow.
8. The shortest stories were theirs.
9. Yours was the funniest story.
10. Ours was the best story time ever.

Interrogative Pronouns

> A pronoun used in asking a question is an interrogative pronoun.
> The interrogative pronouns are: who, what and which.
> **Who** is used in speaking of persons. **What** is used in speaking of things. **Which** is used in speaking of persons or things.
> Who is the only interrogative pronoun that changes form. Who is used as the subject or predicate nominative. When the sentence requires a direct object or an object of a preposition, use whom instead of who. The possessive form of this pronoun is whose.

Underline the interrogative pronouns in each sentence. Tell whether it refers to a person or a thing.

Who(P) knew the answer?

1. For whom(P) will you vote?
2. Whom(P) do you prefer?
3. What(T) are the issues?
4. Which(P) of you will speak first?
5. Which(P) will be the moderator of the debate?
6. Who(P) will count the ballots?
7. This ballot is mine, but whose(P) is this?
8. Who(P) was elected our class representative?
9. To whom(P) will the title be awarded?
10. What(T) are the results of the election?

Page 60

Compound Personal Pronouns   Name _____

> To form compound personal pronouns, add **-self** or **-selves** to certain forms of the personal pronouns.
> First person compound personal pronouns are: myself and ourselves. Second person compound personal pronouns are: yourself and yourselves. Third person compound personal pronouns are: himself, herself, itself and themselves.

Underline the compound personal pronouns in the following sentences.

We helped ourselves to dessert.

1. The instructor said all students must prepare themselves for the examination.
2. He prepared himself for the test by studying carefully.
3. Are you, yourselves, ready?
4. We wrote the practice question ourselves.
5. I, myself, studied two hours.
6. Have you mastered the skills yourself?

Relative Pronouns

> A relative pronoun is one that relates to a noun or pronoun which comes before it. The noun or pronoun that precedes the relative pronoun is called its antecedent.
> The relative pronouns are: who, whom, which and that.
> **Who and whom** relate to persons. **Which** relates to animals or things. **That** relates to persons, animals or things.

Underline the relative pronoun and circle its antecedent.

He could not attend the (schools) that were far away.

1. George Washington Carver was a (boy) who wanted to learn.
2. His life began as a (slave) who lived on a cotton plantation.
3. He was named after (George Washington) who was the first president.
4. The plantation owners gave the boy their own last (name) which was Carver.
5. After the (war) that freed the slaves, George remained with Mr. and Mrs. Carver.
6. George wanted an (education) which would help him in life.
7. Mrs. Carver gave him a (Bible) which he used as a reading textbook.

Uses of Pronouns (Subject)   Name _____

> Pronouns take the place of a noun. A pronoun may be used as the subject in a sentence.
> Subject pronouns: I, you, he, she, it, we, they.

Underline the subject pronouns.

<u>We</u> like gardening in our family.

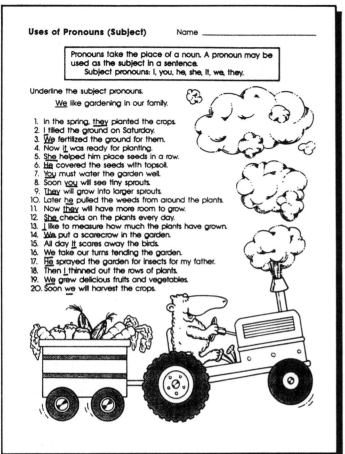

1. In the spring, <u>they</u> planted the crops.
2. <u>I</u> tilled the ground on Saturday.
3. <u>We</u> fertilized the ground for them.
4. Now <u>it</u> was ready for planting.
5. <u>She</u> helped him place seeds in a row.
6. <u>He</u> covered the seeds with topsoil.
7. <u>You</u> must water the garden well.
8. Soon <u>you</u> will see tiny sprouts.
9. <u>They</u> will grow into larger sprouts.
10. Later <u>he</u> pulled the weeds from around the plants.
11. Now <u>they</u> will have more room to grow.
12. <u>She</u> checks on the plants every day.
13. <u>I</u> like to measure how much the plants have grown.
14. <u>We</u> put a scarecrow in the garden.
15. All day <u>it</u> scares away the birds.
16. We take our turns tending the garden.
17. <u>He</u> sprayed the garden for insects for my father.
18. Then <u>I</u> thinned out the rows of plants.
19. <u>We</u> grew delicious fruits and vegetables.
20. Soon <u>we</u> will harvest the crops.

Uses of Pronouns (Direct Object)   Name _____

> A pronoun may be used as the direct object of a verb.
> Object pronouns are: me, you, him, her, it, us, them.

Underline the object pronouns.

We saw <u>it</u> in the newspaper.

1. Six Flags Over Mid-America attracts <u>me</u>.
2. Erica likes <u>it</u>, too.
3. The rides thrill <u>us</u> every time we go!
4. The shows entertained <u>us</u>.
5. We saw <u>them</u> in the afternoon.
6. Have you ever seen <u>them</u>?
7. The actors picked <u>her</u> to come on stage.
8. She saw <u>us</u> in the audience.
9. The audience likes <u>it</u> very much.
10. The boys and girls cheered <u>them</u>.
11. The Time Tunnel scared <u>us</u> most of all.
12. The food satisfied <u>him</u>.
13. We lost <u>her</u> in line.
14. The police found <u>her</u> later.
15. A police dog helped them find <u>her</u>.
16. We wanted to reward <u>it</u> for helping.
17. That incident started <u>us</u>!
18. It disturbed <u>her</u> and made <u>her</u> cry.
19. She followed <u>us</u> closely afterwards.
20. We enjoyed <u>it</u> anyway.

Predicate Pronouns   Name _____

> A pronoun may be used as a predicate pronoun. A predicate pronoun follows a linking verb.
> The predicate pronouns are the same as the subject pronouns.

Draw a circle around the predicate pronoun in each sentence.

It was (I) who wrote this report.

1. The reader of this report is (you).
2. The first pilgrims were (they).
3. The farmer is (he).
4. After many months of travel, this was (it).
5. The crop of corn was (it).
6. The sick woman was (she).
7. The most faithful man was (he).
8. Was the captain (he)?
9. The doctor is (he).
10. The leader of the Mayflower was (he).
11. It was (I) who prepared the food on the ship.
12. The writer is (she) who kept notes during the voyage.
13. The happiest children were (we) in hopes of building a new home.
14. The first volunteers were (they).
15. The best hunter was (he).
16. "It is (I)," exclaimed Governor Bradford.
17. It was the Indians and (I) who planted the corn.
18. The writer of the Bible was (she).
19. It was (I) who farmed that plot of land.
20. The land of Plymouth Rock was (it).

Descriptive Adjectives   Name _____

> An adjective is a word used to describe or limit a noun or pronoun. An adjective that describes a noun or pronoun is called a descriptive adjective.

Underline the descriptive adjectives in these sentences.

The <u>small</u> dog ran down the <u>dark</u> street.

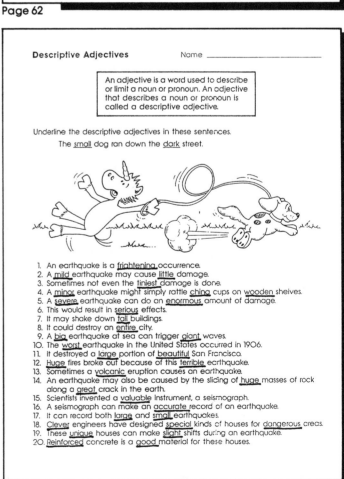

1. An earthquake is a <u>frightening</u> occurrence.
2. A <u>mild</u> earthquake may cause <u>little</u> damage.
3. Sometimes not even the <u>tiniest</u> damage is done.
4. A <u>minor</u> earthquake might simply rattle <u>china</u> cups on <u>wooden</u> shelves.
5. A <u>severe</u> earthquake can do an <u>enormous</u> amount of damage.
6. This would result in <u>serious</u> effects.
7. It may shake down <u>tall</u> buildings.
8. It could destroy an <u>entire</u> city.
9. A <u>big</u> earthquake at sea can trigger <u>giant</u> waves.
10. The <u>worst</u> earthquake in the United States occurred in 1906.
11. It destroyed a <u>large</u> portion of <u>beautiful</u> San Francisco.
12. <u>Huge</u> fires broke out because of this <u>terrible</u> earthquake.
13. Sometimes a <u>volcanic</u> eruption causes an earthquake.
14. An earthquake may also be caused by the sliding of <u>huge</u> masses of rock along a <u>great</u> crack in the earth.
15. Scientists invented a <u>valuable</u> instrument, a seismograph.
16. A seismograph can make an <u>accurate</u> record of an earthquake.
17. It can record both <u>large</u> and <u>small</u> earthquakes.
18. <u>Clever</u> engineers have designed <u>special</u> kinds of houses for <u>dangerous</u> areas.
19. These <u>unique</u> houses can make <u>slight</u> shifts during an earthquake.
20. <u>Reinforced</u> concrete is a <u>good</u> material for these houses.

Answer Key

Descriptive Adjectives   Name _____

> An adjective is a word used to describe or limit a noun or pronoun. An adjective that describes a noun or pronoun is called a descriptive adjective.

Circle the descriptive adjectives and underline the nouns they modify.

The (small) girl read a (big) book.

1. Corals are (tiny) animals that live in (warm) seas.
2. Corals are (simple) animals.
3. They wave food into their (small) mouths with (tiny) feelers.
4. They look like (little) flowers.
5. (New) animals branch off (old) animals.
6. Soon a (large) colony is built.
7. The (small) animals use lime from the water.
8. They build (high) walls around themselves like (big) houses.
9. The (older) animals die.
10. Their (limestone) houses remain.
11. There are (beautiful) corals in the Pacific Ocean.
12. (Huge) reefs rise in (big) circles above the (blue) sea.
13. These (tall) circles of coral are called atolls.
14. There are (different) kinds of coral.
15. They have (various) shapes.
16. Staghorn and sea fan are (common) types of coral.
17. (Precious) coral has a (red) color.
18. (Pretty) beads are made from it.
19. There are (yellow) and (blue) corals.
20. Sea whip has a deep (purple) color.

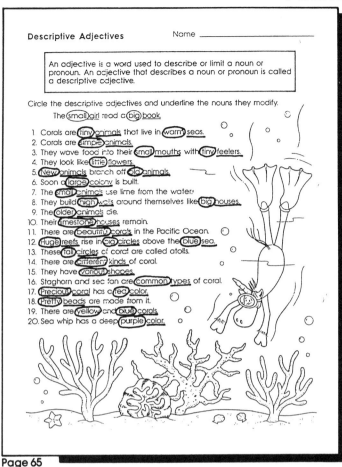

Page 65

Positive Degree of Adjectives   Name _____

> Adjectives change form according to the different degrees of comparison. There are three degrees of comparison: the positive, the comparative and the superlative.
>
> The positive degree indicates quality.

In each sentence, underline the adjective in positive degree.

That is a delightful story.

1. Many people collect fine shells as a hobby.
2. The shell is the hard covering of some animals.
3. Shells make a good protection for the animals that have them.
4. The queen conch is a big shell.
5. This shell has a beautiful lining.
6. The lining has a smooth surface.
7. Some shells have round shapes.
8. Others have flat forms.
9. Other varieties have sharp edges.
10. It is possible to have a shell collection in a small place.
11. Some shells do not have large shapes.
12. Various types of shells have narrow contours.
13. Other shells would take up a great amount of space.
14. Animals with shells have lived in the deep sea for millions of years.
15. Many of the hard shells of these animals have sunk to the bottom of the sea.
16. They have formed thick layers in some places in the ocean.
17. Shells have been important possessions for humans at different times.
18. The American Indians used pretty shells for money.
19. Many tiny beads are made from shells.
20. Lovely buttons can also be made from shells.

Page 66

Comparative Degree of Adjectives   Name _____

> The comparative degree indicates a greater or lesser degree of quality. It is used when comparing two items.

Form the comparative degree for each of the following adjectives.

Positive	Comparative
loud	louder
good	better
1. big	bigger
2. happy	happier
3. useful	more useful
4. small	smaller
5. little	less
6. playful	more playful
7. kind	kinder
8. beautiful	more beautiful
9. large	larger
10. important	more important

Underline the adjectives in the comparative degree.

1. Vegetables are better in our diet than certain snacks.
2. Some vegetables are better sources of certain vitamins that others.
3. Vegetables are more valuable for providing minerals in the diet than some other types of foods.
4. Some vegetables are more delicious cooked.
5. Others are tastier raw.
6. Some vegetables, like squash, are more colorful than others.
7. Corn grows taller than many other vegetables.
8. Tomatoes are usually larger than radishes.
9. Today's methods for raising vegetables are more advanced than those of 100 years ago.
10. However, some vegetables are easier to grow than others.

Page 67

Superlative Degree of Adjectives   Name _____

> The superlative degree indicates the greatest or the least degree of quality. It is used when comparing three or more.

Form the comparative and superlative degrees for each adjective below.

Positive	Comparative	Superlative
light	lighter	lightest
good	better	best
1. much	more	most
2. tall	taller	tallest
3. harmful	more harmful	most harmful
4. difficult	more difficult	most difficult
5. thoughtful	more thoughtful	most thoughtful
6. wide	wider	widest
7. helpful	more helpful	most helpful
8. dark	darker	darkest
9. comfortable	more comfortable	most comfortable
10. bright	brighter	brightest

Underline the adjectives that are compared. Label if they are in the positive, comparative or superlative degree.

Superlative 1. Most parts of the world have four seasons each year.
superlative 2. Summer is usually the hottest season.
Superlative 3. Winter is the coldest time of the year.
positive 4. Spring is generally warm.
comparative 5. In fall, the weather becomes cooler.
comparative 6. The earth is a farther distance from the sun in June than in December.
comparative 7. Summers would be warmer and winters colder in the northern hemisphere if that position were reversed.
positive 8. People often give a simple reason for the changing of the seasons.
comparative 9. Scientific data offers a more complete explanation.

Page 68

Answer Key

Page 69

Limiting Adjectives   Name _____

> A limiting adjective is one which points out an object or indicates number.
> The articles are a, an and the. **The** is a definite article and is used with singular or plural nouns. **A** and **an** are indefinite articles. They are used with singular nouns.

Write the correct indefinite article before each noun.

    _a_ teacher   _an_ author

1. _a_ mountain
2. _an_ advisor
3. _a_ suitcase
4. _a_ painting
5. _an_ instrument
6. _a_ storm
7. _a_ forest
8. _an_ umbrella
9. _an_ example
10. _a_ picnic
11. _a_ machine
12. _an_ award
13. _a_ performance
14. _a_ footprint
15. _an_ hour
16. _a_ contest

> A numeral adjective is one which indicates an exact number such as six, forty or third.

In the following sentences, circle the articles and underline the numeral adjectives.

1. It is hard to imagine (a) time when there wasn't even one book.
2. (The) first books were made in Egypt more than five thousand years ago.
3. (The) first books were not made of pages bound together between (a) cover.
4. Sheets of papyrus were pasted together to form one long strip.
5. One strip was one hundred forty-four feet in length.
6. It took two hands to read such (a) roll book.
7. One hand-written book could take from six months to five years to copy.
8. Five hundred years ago, (a) book collector boasted all his books were "written with (the) pen."
9. Later, two inventions, paper and (the) printing press, changed (the) way books were made.
10. Recently, (a) collector paid five hundred thousand dollars for one copy of (an) early book printed on (the) Guttenberg press.

Page 69

Page 70

Demonstrative Adjectives   Name _____

> **This, that, these** and **those** are adjectives that point out a definite person, place or thing. Use **this** and **these** to point out objects near at hand. Use **that** and **those** to refer to objects at a distance.

Use the proper demonstrative adjective before the following objects which are near at hand.

    this camera   these books

1. this month
2. this bicycle
3. these lamps
4. this house
5. these chairs
6. this team
7. these paintings
8. this flag
9. these girls
10. these shoes
11. these peaches
12. these flowers
13. this piano
14. these cars
15. these dishes
16. this novel
17. these jobs
18. these boxes

Use the proper demonstrative adjective to point out the following objects which are at a distance.

    that home   those mountains

1. those keys
2. that city
3. those buildings
4. those jewels
5. that recipe
6. that plant
7. those cabinets
8. that horse
9. those jars
10. those papers
11. that journey
12. those games
13. that family
14. those leaves
15. that shelf
16. those trees
17. that playground
18. those glasses

Page 70

Page 71

Indefinite Adjectives   Name _____

> An indefinite adjective is one that does not point out any one person, place or thing in particular.
> The indefinite adjectives are: all, another, any, both, few, many, several, some, such and same.

Circle the indefinite adjective and underline the noun it modifies.

    We had (some) fruit for dessert.

1. There are (many) kinds of jobs.
2. (Both) men and women have (many) choices open to them.
3. (Any) decision about a job takes careful thought.
4. (Some) jobs require special training.
5. (Few) jobs require no training.
6. (Several) occupations demand a college education.
7. (Such) requirements are necessary for doctors and lawyers.
8. Teachers also study for (many) years.
9. Counseling is (another) job.
10. This job requires (several) years of study and training.
11. (All) jobs involve (some) kind of mental or physical work.
12. (Such) labor provides (several) choices for workers.
13. Today's work force needs (many) kinds of people.
14. (All) workers should put forth (much) effort.
15. Choose your career from the (many) jobs available.
16. (All) kinds of opportunities await you.
17. (Both) education and enthusiasm are important factors.
18. Perhaps we will choose the (same) career.
19. We hope it will be more than just (another) job.
20. We anticipate (much) satisfaction in the job we choose.

Page 71

Page 72

Possessive Adjectives   Name _____

> A possessive adjective is an adjective which indicates ownership.
> The possessive adjectives are: my, our, your, his, her, its and their.

Circle the possessive adjective and underline the noun it modifies.

    These sentences are about (their) supplies.

1. (His) supplies are on (her) desk.
2. (Their) things had been lost for several days.
3. I keep (my) pencils in a case.
4. Keep (your) papers in a folder.
5. This will help keep (your) things organized.
6. (Her) book had several torn pages.
7. (Its) cover was dirty.
8. I hope (her) book is not ruined.
9. (His) pencil was missing (its) eraser.
10. A friend found (their) missing items.
11. (My) classmate shared (her) crayons with me.
12. (Their) pens were near (your) seat.
13. I was happy we could share (our) markers.
14. (His) bottle of glue is empty.
15. Sharpen (your) pencils now.
16. (Their) scissors are sharp.
17. (Our) reports are on (her) desk.
18. They passed (their) papers forward.
19. (His) project is not finished.
20. We store (our) books on the shelf.

Page 72

Answer Key

Interrogative Adjectives Name _____

> An interrogative adjective is one which is used in asking a question.
> The interrogative adjectives are **what** and **which**.

Circle the interrogative adjective and underline the noun it modifies.

(Which) boy is first?
(What) time will you leave?

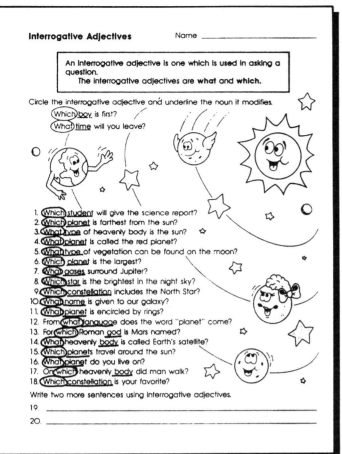

1. (Which) student will give the science report?
2. (Which) planet is farthest from the sun?
3. (What) type of heavenly body is the sun?
4. (What) planet is called the red planet?
5. (What) type of vegetation can be found on the moon?
6. (Which) planet is the largest?
7. (What) gases surround Jupiter?
8. (Which) star is the brightest in the night sky?
9. (Which) constellation includes the North Star?
10. (What) name is given to our galaxy?
11. (What) planet is encircled by rings?
12. From (what) language does the word "planet" come?
13. For (which) Roman god is Mars named?
14. (What) heavenly body is called Earth's satellite?
15. (Which) planets travel around the sun?
16. (What) planet do you live on?
17. On (which) heavenly body did man walk?
18. (Which) constellation is your favorite?

Write two more sentences using interrogative adjectives.

19. _____
20. _____

Page 73

Predicate Adjectives Name _____

> A predicate adjective follows a linking verb and completes the meaning of the verb.

Underline the linking verb and circle the predicate adjective.

The meal was (delicious.)

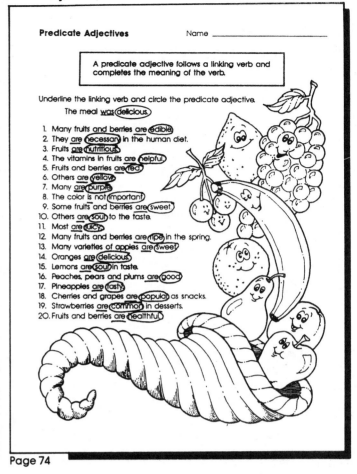

1. Many fruits and berries are (edible.)
2. They are (necessary) in the human diet.
3. Fruits are (nutritious.)
4. The vitamins in fruits are (helpful.)
5. Fruits and berries are (red.)
6. Others are (yellow.)
7. Many are (purple.)
8. The color is not (important.)
9. Some fruits and berries are (sweet.)
10. Others are (sour) to the taste.
11. Most are (juicy.)
12. Many fruits and berries are (ripe) in the spring.
13. Many varieties of apples are (sweet.)
14. Oranges are (delicious.)
15. Lemons are (sour) in taste.
16. Peaches, pears and plums are (good.)
17. Pineapples are (tasty.)
18. Cherries and grapes are (popular) as snacks.
19. Strawberries are (common) in desserts.
20. Fruits and berries are (healthful.)

Page 74

Prepositions Name _____

> A preposition is a word used to show the relationship of a noun or a pronoun to some other word in a sentence.
> A preposition is placed before a noun or pronoun. This noun or pronoun becomes the object of the preposition.

Circle the preposition and underline its object.

The car raced (around) the track.

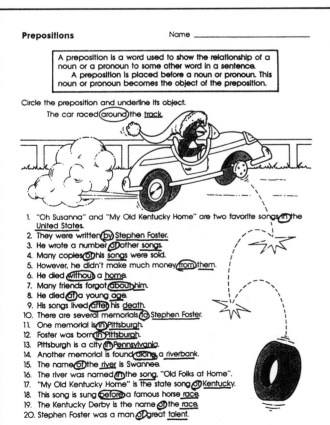

1. "Oh Susanna" and "My Old Kentucky Home" are two favorite songs (in) the United States.
2. They were written (by) Stephen Foster.
3. He wrote a number (of) other songs.
4. Many copies (of) his songs were sold.
5. However, he didn't make much money (from) them.
6. He died (without) a home.
7. Many friends forgot (about) him.
8. He died (at) a young age.
9. His songs lived (after) his death.
10. There are several memorials (to) Stephen Foster.
11. One memorial is (in) Pittsburgh.
12. Foster was born (in) Pittsburgh.
13. Pittsburgh is a city (in) Pennsylvania.
14. Another memorial is found (along) a riverbank.
15. The name (of) the river is Swannee.
16. The river was named (in) the song, "Old Folks at Home".
17. "My Old Kentucky Home" is the state song (of) Kentucky.
18. This song is sung (before) a famous horse race.
19. The Kentucky Derby is the name (of) the race.
20. Stephen Foster was a man (of) great talent.

Page 75

Prepositions Name _____

> A preposition is a word used to show the relationship of a noun or a pronoun to some other word in a sentence.
> A preposition is placed before a noun or pronoun. This noun or pronoun becomes the object of the preposition.

Circle the preposition and underline its object.

The boat sailed (across) the ocean.

1. Young Walter Reed lived (in) Virginia.
2. He entered the University (of) Virginia.
3. Medicine was his area (of) study.
4. He became the youngest medical graduate (from) the school.
5. Later, he became a doctor (for) the army.
6. He was stationed (in) Arizona.
7. He doctored the soldiers (in) the garrison.
8. Reed also helped the other people (in) the region.
9. Fourteen years later, Reed was sent (to) Baltimore.
10. There he studied (at) John Hopkins University.
11. Soon he became a professor (at) the Army Medical School.
12. His experiments proved the reason (for) typhoid fever.
13. Germs (from) flies caused the disease.
14. Yellow fever was another problem (for) soldiers.
15. Reed and several other army doctors went (to) Cuba.
16. They studied possible causes (of) the disease.
17. Their information pointed (to) mosquitoes.
18. Killing mosquitoes there brought an end (to) yellow fever.
19. This also worked (in) the United States.
20. Our government named a large army hospital (for) Walter Reed.

Page 76

Answer Key

Page 77

Adjectival Phrases   Name _____

An adjectival phrase is a group of words used as an adjective. The phrase begins with a preposition.

Underline the adjectival phrase and circle the noun it modifies.

An (evening) with shooting stars is exciting.

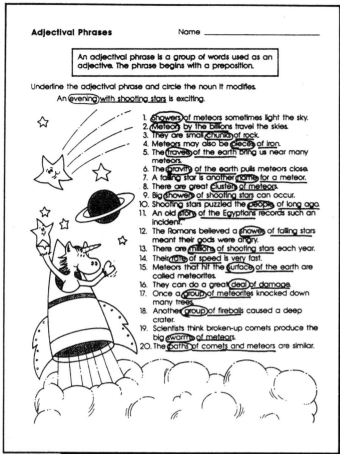

1. (Showers) of meteors sometimes light the sky.
2. (Meteors) by the billions travel the skies.
3. They are small (chunks) of rock.
4. Meteors may also be (pieces) of iron.
5. The (travels) of the earth bring us near many meteors.
6. The (gravity) of the earth pulls meteors close.
7. A falling (star) is another (name) for a meteor.
8. There are great (clusters) of meteors.
9. Big (showers) of shooting stars can occur.
10. Shooting stars puzzled the (people) of long ago.
11. An old (story) of the Egyptians records such an incident.
12. The Romans believed a (shower) of falling stars meant their gods were angry.
13. There are (millions) of shooting stars each year.
14. Their (rate) of speed is very fast.
15. Meteors that hit the (surface) of the earth are called meteorites.
16. They can do a great (deal) of damage.
17. Once a (group) of meteorites knocked down many trees.
18. Another (group) of fireballs caused a deep crater.
19. Scientists think broken-up comets produce the big (swarms) of meteors.
20. The (paths) of comets and meteors are similar.

Page 77

Page 78

Adjectival Phrases   Name _____

An adjectival phrase is a group of words used as an adjective. The phrase begins with a preposition.

Underline the adjectival phrase and circle the noun it modifies.

She has a large (collection) of shells.

1. Marie Curie is an important (name) in science.
2. She was a (girl) of great intelligence.
3. Once, she received a gold (medal) for her good work.
4. She was a college (student) with little money.
5. Marie's (life) at college was difficult.
6. The (desire) for knowledge inspired her.
7. Pierre Curie was a (scientist) of great ability.
8. Their marriage began a (partnership) for a lifetime.
9. Long (hours) of hard work marked their years together.
10. The (discovery) of radium was recorded.
11. Eventually their (work) with radium was successful.
12. The discovery was a major (breakthrough) in scientific research.
13. The powerful (effects) of radium could help sick people.
14. (Experiments) with this element continued.
15. Many (people) of importance praised Pierre and Marie Curie.
16. Their (dedication) to science did not change.
17. Pierre's death was the (end) of their happy marriage.
18. Marie continued her (experiments) with radium.
19. Too much (exposure) to radium caused Marie's death.
20. The (accomplishments) of these two scientists will never be forgotten.

Page 78

Page 79

Adverbial Phrases   Name _____

An adverbial phrase is a group of words used as an adverb. A preposition begins an adverbial phrase.

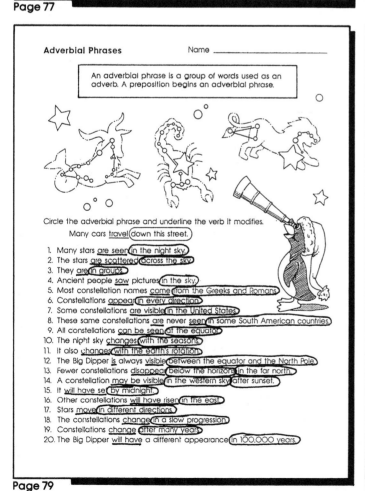

Circle the adverbial phrase and underline the verb it modifies.

Many cars travel (down this street.)

1. Many stars are seen (in the night sky.)
2. The stars are scattered (across the sky.)
3. They are (in groups.)
4. Ancient people saw pictures (in the sky.)
5. Most constellation names come (from the Greeks and Romans.)
6. Constellations appear (in every direction.)
7. Some constellations are visible (in the United States.)
8. These same constellations are never seen (in some South American countries.)
9. All constellations can be seen (at the equator.)
10. The night sky changes (with the seasons.)
11. It also changes (with the earth's rotation.)
12. The Big Dipper is always visible (between the equator and the North Pole.)
13. Fewer constellations disappear (below the horizon) (in the far north.)
14. A constellation may be visible (in the western sky) (after sunset.)
15. It will have set (by midnight.)
16. Other constellations will have risen (in the east.)
17. Stars move (in different directions.)
18. The constellations change (in a slow progression.)
19. Constellations change (after many years.)
20. The Big Dipper will have a different appearance (in 100,000 years.)

Page 79

Page 80

Adverbial Phrases   Name _____

An adverbial phrase is a group of words used as an adverb. A preposition begins an adverbial phrase.

Circle the adverbial phrase and underline the verb it modifies.

Many people live (in Spain.)

1. Spain is located (in southern Europe.)
2. Spanish power increased (with a wedding.)
3. Princess Isabella and Prince Ferdinand married (in 1469.)
4. Columbus sailed (under the Spanish flag.)
5. He journeyed (across the Atlantic Ocean.)
6. The Spanish king and queen hoped (for wealth.)
7. New lands were claimed (in 1492.)
8. Great riches were brought (from the New World.)
9. The Spanish empire grew (in size.)
10. Spain's power decreased (with the navy's defeat.)
11. Most Spanish colonies were lost (by the nineteenth century.)
12. Napoleon ruled Spain (for a time.)
13. Spain has had many governments (since Napoleon.)
14. A revolt occurred (in 1936.)
15. It was fought (against the government.)
16. A civil war raged (in Spain.)
17. This lasted (for three years.)
18. Francisco Franco became Spain's leader (after the war.)
19. Today there is a king (in Spain) once more.
20. Spain's progress has developed (through the years.)

Page 80

Answer Key

Page 81

Adverbs of Time Name _____

> An adverb is a word that modifies a verb, an adjective or another adverb. Adverbs may indicate time, place or manner.
> Adverbs of Time answer the questions **when** or **how often**. They usually modify verbs.

Circle the Adverbs of Time and underline the verbs they modify.

My friends <u>meet</u> here (often).

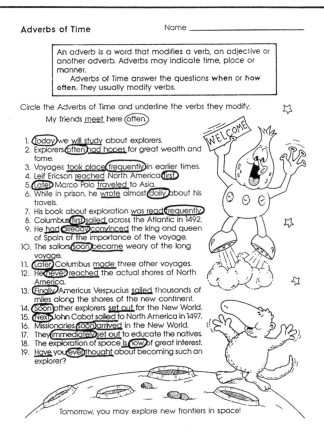

1. (Today) we will <u>study</u> about explorers.
2. Explorers (often) <u>had hopes</u> for great wealth and fame.
3. Voyages <u>took place</u> (frequently) in earlier times.
4. Leif Ericson <u>reached</u> North America (first).
5. (Later) Marco Polo <u>traveled</u> to Asia.
6. While in prison, he <u>wrote</u> almost (daily) about his travels.
7. His book about exploration <u>was read</u> (frequently).
8. Columbus (first) <u>sailed</u> across the Atlantic in 1492.
9. He had (already) <u>convinced</u> the king and queen of Spain of the importance of the voyage.
10. The sailors (soon) <u>became</u> weary of the long voyage.
11. (Later) Columbus <u>made</u> three other voyages.
12. He (never) <u>reached</u> the actual shores of North America.
13. (Finally) Americus Vespucius <u>sailed</u> thousands of miles along the shores of the new continent.
14. (Soon) other explorers <u>set out</u> for the New World.
15. (Next) John Cabot <u>sailed</u> to North America in 1497.
16. Missionaries (soon) <u>arrived</u> in the New World.
17. They (immediately) <u>set out</u> to educate the natives.
18. The exploration of space <u>is</u> (now) of great interest.
19. <u>Have</u> you (ever) <u>thought</u> about becoming such an explorer?

Tomorrow, you may explore new frontiers in space!

Page 81

Page 82

Adverbs of Time Name _____

> An adverb is a word that modifies a verb, an adjective or another adverb. Adverbs may indicate time, place or manner.
> Adverbs of Time answer the questions **when** or **how often**. They usually modify verbs.

Circle the Adverbs of Time and underline the verbs they modify.

<u>Do</u> your homework (first).

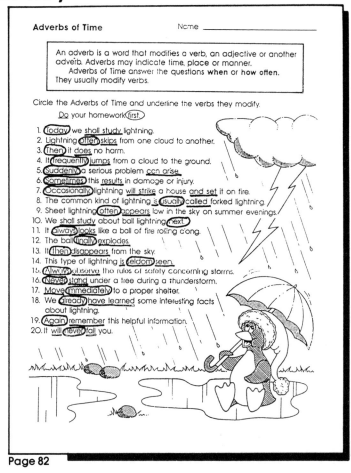

1. (Today) we shall <u>study</u> lightning.
2. Lightning (often) <u>skips</u> from one cloud to another.
3. (Then) it <u>does</u> no harm.
4. It (frequently) <u>jumps</u> from a cloud to the ground.
5. (Suddenly) a serious problem <u>can arise</u>.
6. (Sometimes) this <u>results</u> in damage or injury.
7. (Occasionally) lightning <u>will strike</u> a house <u>and set</u> it on fire.
8. The common kind of lightning <u>is</u> (usually) <u>called</u> forked lightning.
9. Sheet lightning (often) <u>appears</u> low in the sky on summer evenings.
10. We shall <u>study</u> about ball lightning (next).
11. It (always) <u>looks</u> like a ball of fire rolling along.
12. The ball (finally) <u>explodes</u>.
13. It (then) <u>disappears</u> from the sky.
14. This type of lightning <u>is</u> (seldom) <u>seen</u>.
15. (Always) <u>observe</u> the rules of safety concerning storms.
16. (Never) <u>stand</u> under a tree during a thunderstorm.
17. <u>Move</u> (immediately) to a proper shelter.
18. We (already) <u>have learned</u> some interesting facts about lightning.
19. (Again) <u>remember</u> this helpful information.
20. It will (never) <u>fail</u> you.

Page 82

Page 83

Adverbs of Place Name _____

> Adverbs of Place answer the question **where**. They usually modify verbs.

Circle the Adverb of Place and underline the verbs they modify.

The kitten <u>darted</u> (away).

1. The sentences (here) <u>will tell</u> about geysers.
2. The eruption of a geyser <u>sends</u> (forth) gushes of water.
3. The geyser <u>shoots</u> water (up) into the air.
4. There <u>must be</u> hot rock not (far) below the ground.
5. A narrow, crooked passage <u>must lead</u> (up) from the hot rock.
6. The crooked passage <u>is filled</u> (in) with water.
7. Hot water is <u>held</u> (here).
8. The boiling water at the bottom of the passage <u>forms</u> steam (within).
9. The steam <u>pushes</u> (out) the cooler water at the top of the passage.
10. A little of this water <u>comes</u> (out).
11. Then less cold water <u>pushes</u> (down) on the hot water.
12. Steam <u>forms</u> (below).
13. The steam <u>shoots</u> the water (upward).
14. The water <u>soars</u> (above).
15. People <u>must stand</u> (back).
16. Geysers <u>are</u> not <u>formed</u> (everywhere) around the world.
17. Old Faithful <u>is found</u> (here) in Yellowstone National Park.
18. It <u>erupts</u> (there) every 65 minutes.
19. Few people <u>go</u> (away) disappointed by the wait.
20. Other geysers <u>are found</u> (far) from the U.S. in Iceland and Greenland.

Page 83

Page 84

Adverbs of Place Name _____

> Adverbs of Place answer the question **where**. They usually modify verbs.

Circle the Adverb of Place and underline the verbs they modify.

The dog <u>ran</u> (away).

1. The sentences (below) <u>are</u> about lakes.
2. Lakes <u>are located</u> (everywhere) around the world.
3. Water <u>runs</u> (in) and (out) of fresh-water lakes.
4. Water <u>runs</u> (down) from the slope of the land.
5. The source of the water <u>starts</u> (above).
6. Some large fresh-water lakes <u>are</u> (here) in our country.
7. Water <u>flows</u> (in) but not (out) of saltwater lakes.
8. Saltwater lakes <u>are found</u> (here) in dry regions.
9. One saltwater lake, the Caspian Sea, <u>is</u> (far) from the United States.
10. Water in lakes <u>evaporates</u> (upward).
11. All salt in saltwater lakes <u>stays</u> (there).
12. Plants <u>spread</u> (out) from the shores of some lakes.
13. Several lakes <u>are situated</u> (high) above sea level.

Fill in an Adverb of Place to complete each sentence. Use words from the list.

down	outside	overhead	there	away

1. You may play *outside*.
2. The bird flew *away*.
3. The little girl fell *down*.
4. The mailman left the package *there*.
5. Fluffy clouds floated *overhead*.

Page 84

Answer Key

Page 85

Adverbs of Manner   Name _____

> Adverbs of Manner answer the question how or in what manner. They usually modify verbs.

Circle the Adverbs of Manner and underline the verbs they modify.

Drive the car carefully.

1. The game of baseball is easily considered the national sport of the United States.
2. In 1839, Abner Doubleday carefully laid out the first baseball diamond in Cooperstown, N.Y.
3. Baseball simply grew out of earlier types of games.
4. Baseballs and bats are made precisely.
5. They must fit the specifications of the rules exactly.
6. Players work hard during practice sessions.
7. They must run swiftly around the bases.
8. They also gracefully demonstrate many fielding skills.
9. These professionals play the game expertly.
10. Most people understand the game well.
11. People cheerfully await the beginning of the baseball season.
12. The fans cheer loudly for the team of their choice.
13. The game moves fast through nine innings.
14. Time passes slowly when the other team is winning.
15. At the end of the baseball season, the winners of the National League and the American League eagerly play the World Series.

Fill in an Adverb of Manner to complete each sentence. Use words from the list below.

| quickly | carefully | neatly | bravely | kindly |

1. Please arrange the books **neatly** on the shelves.
2. The ice cream melted **quickly** in the hot sun.
3. Always speak **kindly** to others.
4. The soldiers fought **bravely** for their country.
5. Do your work **carefully** at all times.

Page 86

Comparison of Adverbs   Name _____

> Many adverbs may be compared. They have three degrees of comparison: positive, comparative and superlative.

Complete each of the following comparisons.

POSITIVE	COMPARATIVE	SUPERLATIVE
fast	faster	fastest
bravely	most bravely	most bravely
much	more	most
1. far	farther	farthest
2. quickly	more quickly	most quickly
3. hard	harder	hardest
4. well	better	best
5. slowly	more slowly	most slowly
6. early	earlier	earliest
7. little	littler	littlest
8. soon	sooner	soonest
9. badly	more badly	most badly
10. happily	more happily	most happily

Underline the adverbs and tell the degree of comparison.

P 1. Machines are used to do work easily.
P 2. Any type of machinery should be operated carefully.
C 3. A machine can do some work more efficiently than a person.
C 4. Some types of machinery are used to move objects more quickly.
P 5. A farmer uses a large combine to harvest his crops swiftly.
S 6. Computers can keep records most accurately.
C 7. With the development of machines, factories were built more hurriedly.
P 8. Cities grew fast.
S 9. Most probably people would not want to do without machines.

Page 87

Correct Use of Adverbs   Name _____

> Adjectives modify nouns and pronouns. Adverbs modify verbs, adjectives or other adverbs. If the verb in the sentence is a linking verb, or if any form of the verb be can be substituted for the verb in the sentence, use an adjective. If the verb be cannot be substituted, use an adverb.

Choose the correct word in each sentence.

Daniel did the work (good, **well**).
His work is (**good**, well).

1. Justice is shown as a blindfolded woman (calm, **calmly**) holding a balance.
2. The reason for the scales is (**easy**, easily) to understand.
3. One must listen (careful, **carefully**) to both sides of a disagreement.
4. Justice must exercise fairness (complete, **completely**).
5. Since the beginning of man, some individuals have been treated (unfair, **unfairly**) by others.
6. Some early rulers settled disputes (clever, **cleverly**).
7. In ancient times, the leader of the tribe (usual, **usually**) decided guilt or innocence.
8. Certain stories of some early disputes are (**true**, truly).
9. One of these stories is about how King Solomon (wise, **wisely**) settled a question concerning a child.
10. King Solomon was (**just**, justly).
11. More than a few rulers became (**famous**, famously).
12. In many cases they acted (brave, **bravely**).
13. (Gradual, **Gradually**), courts of law came to settle disputes.
14. In many countries, courts are (full, **fully**) responsible for such decisions.
15. Judges and juries must be (**honest**, honestly).
16. They decide if a person is (**guilty**, guiltily).
17. This method is considered (**good**, well).
18. Deciding a case may not be (**easy**, easily).
19. Our courts (genuine, **genuinely**) work for justice for all.
20. The people's desire for justice is (**great**, greatly).

Page 88

Interjections   Name _____

> An interjection is a word that expresses strong emotion.

Underline the interjection in each sentence.

1. Bravo! Here comes the parade.
2. Good! I can hardly wait.
3. That marching band is great. Wow!
4. The jugglers are next. Look!
5. Ah! The floats are beautiful.
6. Our school band is next. Hurrah!
7. Indeed! They played their best.
8. Ha! Ha! Watch the clowns.
9. That was quite a parade. Whew!
10. Good-bye! I'll meet you at school tomorrow.

Place an interjection before each sentence. Use the list below. Do not use a word more than once.

What	Ouch
Alas	Hush
Listen	Oh
Beware	Bah
Hello	Good

1. **Beware**! That step is shaky.
2. **Alas**! I broke the vase.
3. **Hush**! You must not talk now.
4. **What**! Did we win the contest?
5. **Oh**! I forgot my money.
6. **Bah**! That is terrible.
7. **Hello**! Is that you?
8. **Ouch**! I scraped my knee.
9. **Listen**! I heard a noise.
10. **Good**! You arrived just in time.

Answer Key

Interjections   Name _____

> An interjection is a word that expresses strong emotion.

Underline the interjection in each sentence.

1. <u>Oh!</u> Here come the two teams.
2. <u>Hush!</u> The contest has begun.
3. Did you hear his answer? <u>Listen!</u>
4. Her answer was wrong. <u>Alas!</u>
5. <u>Good!</u> Our team is ahead.
6. That is a tricky question. <u>Beware!</u>
7. <u>Great!</u> Our team has one last chance.
8. That was good teamwork. <u>Bravo!</u>
9. <u>Hurray!</u> Our class won the contest.
10. <u>Wow!</u> The trophy is big.

1ST. PLACE

Answers will vary.
Add an interjection before each sentence.

1. _____ ! It is raining hard.
2. _____ ! The baby is sleeping.
3. _____ ! That dog is dangerous.
4. _____ ! We won the baseball game.
5. _____ ! This rose is beautiful.
6. _____ ! The cold drink was refreshing.
7. _____ ! I thought I heard a noise.
8. _____ ! My name is Colleen.
9. _____ ! You completed the work.
10. _____ ! I'll see you later.

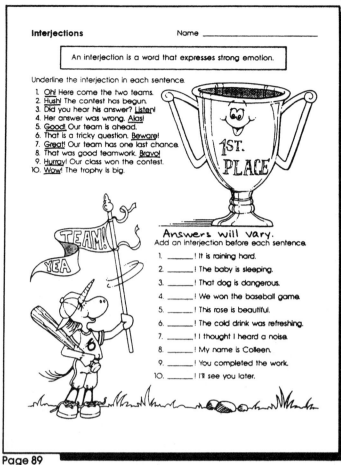

TEAM! YEA

Conjunctions   Name _____

> A conjunction is a word that joins words or groups of words in a sentence.

In each sentence, circle the conjunctions.

Gold (and) silver are valuable.
We may travel by plane (or) by train.
Christine went on the trip (but) I stayed home.

1. Pine trees and fir trees (are) conifers.
2. Most conifers produce their seeds in cones (or) fruits.
3. Conifers can be trees (or) bushes.
4. Some junipers are short (but) hardy bushes.
5. The redwoods (and) sequoias are the giants of the plant world.
6. Conifers can be found in the United States (and) in other countries.
7. Unlike elms (and) maples, most conifers do not drop their leaves in winter.
8. Larches (and) bald cypresses are conifers.
9. They are conifers, (but) they are not evergreens.
10. Conifers can have scalelike leaves (or) narrow needles.
11. The needles can be different in length (and) in color.
12. They may be flat (or) four-sided in shape.
13. The needles may grow in bunches of two (or) more.
14. Millions (and) millions of conifers have been cut for lumber.
15. At Christmas time, conifers play a big part in our celebrations (and) decorations.
16. Many conifers have been killed by fires (or) disease.
17. Fires can occur by accident (or) on purpose.
18. We must plant (and) protect new trees.
19. They must be allowed to grow (and) mature.
20. Then there will be plenty of conifers (and) evergreens for the future.

Conjunctions   Name _____

> A conjunction is a word that joins words or groups of words in a sentence.

In each sentence, circle the conjunction and underline the words or groups of words it connects.

We tell time by <u>hours</u> (and) <u>minutes.</u>
Corn grows <u>in Canada</u> (and) <u>in the United States.</u>
<u>They traveled to Florida,</u> (but) <u>we went to New York.</u>

1. Trade had its beginnings in <u>marketplaces</u> (and) <u>at fairs.</u>
2. Churches permitted <u>buying</u> (and) <u>selling</u> in their churchyards.
3. During the Middle Ages, Lords allowed <u>markets</u> (and) <u>fairs</u> to be held.
4. <u>Peddlers</u> (and) <u>craftsmen</u> sold their wares in these marketplaces.
5. Great fairs were held each year in <u>cities</u> (and) <u>in towns.</u>
6. The fairs at <u>London</u> (and) <u>Stonebridge</u> in England were famous.
7. Fairs were held in <u>Paris</u> (and) <u>Lyons</u> in France.
8. <u>Spices</u> (and) <u>cloth</u> were for sale along with the many other items.
9. <u>The big fairs were held each year,</u> (but) <u>they were not held at the same time.</u>
10. The fairs were <u>gay</u> (and) <u>festive</u> occasions.
11. <u>Jugglers</u> (and) <u>fortune tellers</u> made the fairs fun.
12. Fairs do not have the same <u>importance</u> (or) <u>purpose</u> they once had.
13. In the United States, there are many <u>state</u> (and) <u>county</u> fairs.
14. These fairs are important to <u>farmers</u> (and) <u>ranchers.</u>
15. Often <u>clubs</u> (and) <u>schools</u> have exhibits.
16. Carnival <u>rides</u> (and) <u>races</u> help everyone have a good time.
17. Vendors shout about the <u>trinkets</u> (and) <u>foods</u> for sale.
18. A world's fair may be held in one <u>city</u> (or) <u>another.</u>
19. Many countries send exhibits to show their progress in <u>science</u> (or) <u>in art.</u>
20. Displays in <u>technology</u> (and) <u>industry</u> are also of great interest.

FOR SALE TRADE

Use of the Comma in a Series, with Dates and Geographic Names   Name _____

> *Commas are used to separate words in a series.
>   The map shows cities, states, rivers and mountains.
>   Commas are used to set off parts of geographical names and dates.
>   Stephanie lived in St. Louis, Missouri.
>   Man landed on the moon on July 20, 1969.

Insert commas where they are needed in the following sentences.

1. The four largest countries in the world are Russia, Canada, China and the United States.
2. The Pilgrims landed in America in December, 1620.
3. The Mississippi River flows into the Gulf of Mexico at New Orleans, Louisiana.
4. Wheat, corn, rice and oats are kinds of cereals.
5. The United States declared independence on July 4, 1776.
6. The Golden Gate Bridge is in San Francisco, California.
7. Vegetable gardens may contain lettuce, tomatoes, beans and onions.
8. Baseball, tennis and golf are popular summer sports.
9. The coldest day on record was August 24, 1960, in Vostok Station Antarctica with a temperature of -127° Fahrenheit.
10. On September 22, 1863, President Lincoln signed the Emancipation Proclamation.
11. Washington, Adams, Jefferson and Madison were the first four presidents.
12. Buckingham Palace is in London, England.
13. Tulips, roses, lilies and daisies can be found in most flower gardens.
14. President John F. Kennedy was assassinated on November 22, 1963.
15. Asia, Africa, Europe, North America, South America, Australia and Antarctica are the seven continents.
16. The Constitution of the United States was adopted on September 17, 1787.
17. Four basic operations in mathematics are addition, subtraction, multiplication and division.
18. The hottest day on record was September 13, 1922, in Al' Aziziyah Libya with a temperature of 136° Fahrenheit.

* In some textbooks, a comma is placed before the and.

Direct Quotations Name _____

Quotation marks are used before and after the exact words spoken by a person. Commas are used to set off short direct quotations, unless a quote is an interrogative or exclamatory sentence. Then a question mark or an exclamation point would be used after the quote.

  Mother said, "You may attend the game."
  "You may go," said Mother, "but be home for dinner."
  "What time is dinner?" Mike asked. "How much fun we had!" he exclaimed.

Supply quotations marks, commas, question marks or exclamation points when they are needed.

1. The librarian said, "Please be quiet."
2. "Hush!" scolded Father.
3. "Can't you see that people are studying?" he whispered.
4. "I'm sorry I disturbed them," I said.
5. "You should have known better," he said, "than to talk out loud."
6. "Where are the reference books?" Father asked the librarian.
7. The woman replied, "They are on the second floor."
8. "Thank you," said Father.
9. "Will you help me find the book I need?" I asked him.
10. "Yes," Father said, "you can count on my help."
11. "The sign says the reference section is to the left," I said.
12. "You're right," he smiled.
13. "We can sit at this table," I offered, "when I write my report."
14. Father said, "I'll read this book while you are working."
15. "It's nearly time to leave," Father reminded me, "because the library will be closing soon."
16. "I'm almost finished with the assignment," I answered.
17. "Thank you for your assistance," I said to the librarian as we left.
18. "What a profitable trip to the library!" Father remarked.

Synonyms Name _____

Synonyms are words that generally have the same meaning.

Match the synonyms in Column A with Column B.

Column A		Column B
g	1. mercy	a tedious
d	2. pity	b defend
k	3. happy	c silly
b	4. protect	d sympathy
c	5. foolish	e risk
a	6. tiresome	f associates
i	7. sparkling	g compassion
m	8. friends	h center
f	9. employees	i glittering
h	10. midst	j place
n	11. catch	k cheerful
j	12. put	l crowd
e	13. peril	m companions
o	14. dark	n grab
l	15. group	o dim

Answers may vary.
Fill in the blanks with pairs of words from above.

1. He showed me great **mercy** and **compassion** when I was feeling bad.
2. Mary was very **foolish** and **silly** for riding on that wild horse.
3. The building was **dark** and **dim**.
4. The assignment was extremely **tiresome** and **tedious**.
5. We must **protect** and **defend** our rights at all times.

(thought bubbles: funny, humorous)

Antonyms Name _____

Antonyms are words that mean the opposite.

Match the antonyms in Column A with Column B.

Column A		Column B
g	1. friend	a innocent
c	2. soldier	b absent
j	3. calm	c civilian
a	4. guilty	d narrow
e	5. dark	e light
b	6. present	f bad
h	7. full	g enemy
d	8. wide	h empty
f	9. good	i quickly
m	10. pretty	j unruly
i	11. slowly	k cold
q	12. answered	l bright
k	13. hot	m ugly
l	14. dull	n descended
r	15. barren	o stale
n	16. ascended	p pazy
o	17. fresh	q asked
p	18. ambitious	r fruitful

Answers may vary.
Fill in the blanks with pairs of words from above.

1. A person should be considered **innocent** until proven **guilty**.
2. It is better to have a person as a **friend** than an **enemy**.
3. If you are **lazy** instead of **ambitious**, you may not succeed.
4. The trees were **full** and not **empty**.
5. The entire class was **present** and not **absent**.

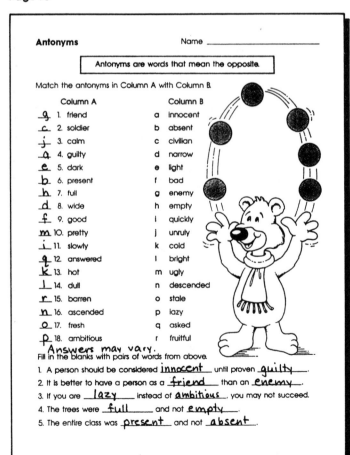

Synonyms and Antonyms Name _____

Synonyms are words with the same or nearly the same meaning.
  talk – speak
Antonyms are words which are opposite in meanings.
  true – false   short – long

Match the pairs of synonyms by writing the letter of the word in Column B in front of the matching synonym in Column A.

Column A		Column B
i	empty	a. pardon
c	answer	b. concealed
a	excuse	c. reply
j	short	d. display
g	hire	e. collect
d	show	f. discovered
e	gather	g. employ
f	invented	h. large
b	hidden	i. vacant
h	great	j. brief

Match the pairs of antonyms by writing the letters of the word in Column B in front of its antonym in Column A.

Column A		Column B
f	wide	a. dull
g	before	b. noisy
b	quiet	c. idle
j	careful	d. cool
h	absent	e. take
d	warm	f. narrow
a	sharp	g. behind
e	give	h. present
i	wild	i. tame
c	busy	j. careless

Select the synonym for the words in parenthesis for each underlined word in the sentence.

1. The answer to the question was wrong. (right, incorrect, incomplete)
2. She is a clever girl. (pretty, silly, smart)
3. Baseball is an exciting game. (display, sport, show)
4. The doctor was gentle with the sick child. (kind, stern, impatient)
5. Let him help you with the problem. (request, ask, allow)

Select the antonym for the words in parenthesis for each underlined word in the sentence.

1. I always anticipate the first day of school. (opening, last, next)
2. This garden tool is useful. (helpful, broken, useless)
3. Put the package there. (near, here, away)
4. She usually arrives early for the show. (late, first, last)
5. He always completes his work on time. (almost, surely, never)

                       © 1990 Instructional Fair, Inc.

Answer Key

Page 97

Homonyms Name _____

> Homonyms are words that sound alike but differ in meaning.

Match the homonyms in Column A with Column B.

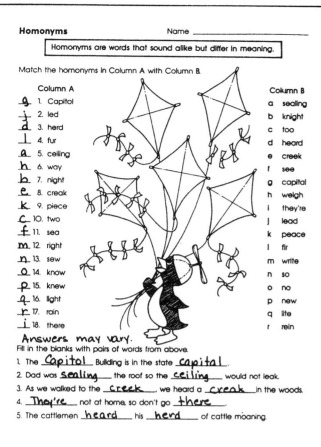

Column A		Column B	
g	1. Capitol	a	sealing
j	2. led	b	knight
d	3. herd	c	too
l	4. fur	d	heard
a	5. ceiling	e	creek
h	6. way	f	see
b	7. night	g	capital
e	8. creak	h	weigh
k	9. piece	i	they're
c	10. two	j	lead
f	11. sea	k	peace
m	12. right	l	fir
n	13. sew	m	write
o	14. know	n	so
p	15. knew	o	no
q	16. light	p	new
r	17. rain	q	lite
i	18. there	r	rein

Answers may vary.
Fill in the blanks with pairs of words from above.

1. The **Capitol** Building is in the state **capital**.
2. Dad was **sealing** the roof so the **ceiling** would not leak.
3. As we walked to the **creek**, we heard a **creak** in the woods.
4. **They're** not at home, so don't go **there**.
5. The cattlemen **heard** his **herd** of cattle moaning.

Page 97

Page 98

Homonyms Name _____

> Homonyms are words which sound alike but have different spellings and different meanings.

In the following sentences choose the correct homonym and write it in the blank.

Their house is around the corner from us. (their, there)

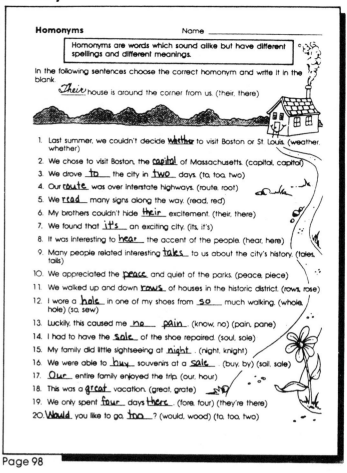

1. Last summer, we couldn't decide **whether** to visit Boston or St. Louis. (weather, whether)
2. We chose to visit Boston, the **capital** of Massachusetts. (capital, capitol)
3. We drove **to** the city in **two** days. (to, too, two)
4. Our **route** was over interstate highways. (route, root)
5. We **read** many signs along the way. (read, red)
6. My brothers couldn't hide **their** excitement. (their, there)
7. We found that **it's** an exciting city. (its, it's)
8. It was interesting to **hear** the accent of the people. (hear, here)
9. Many people related interesting **tales** to us about the city's history. (tales, tails)
10. We appreciated the **peace** and quiet of the parks. (peace, piece)
11. We walked up and down **rows** of houses in the historic district. (rows, rose)
12. I wore a **hole** in one of my shoes from **so** much walking. (whole, hole) (so, sew)
13. Luckily, this caused me **no** **pain**. (know, no) (pain, pane)
14. I had to have the **sole** of the shoe repaired. (soul, sole)
15. My family did little sightseeing at **night**. (night, knight)
16. We were able to **buy** souvenirs at a **sale**. (buy, by) (sail, sale)
17. **Our** entire family enjoyed the trip. (our, hour)
18. This was a **great** vacation. (great, grate)
19. We only spent **four** days **there**. (fore, four) (they're, there)
20. **Would** you like to go, **too**? (would, wood) (to, too, two)

Page 98

Page 99

Contractions Name _____

> A contraction is a shortened form of two or more words. An apostrophe is used in a contraction to show where a letter or letters have been left out.

Write the words from which these contractions are made:

1. they're **they are**
2. can't **can not**
3. hasn't **has not**
4. it's **it is**
5. won't **will not**
6. doesn't **does not**
7. wouldn't **would not**
8. you'll **you will**
9. we've **we have**
10. don't **do not**

Write the contractions for the following words:

1. have not **haven't**
2. of the clock **o'clock**
3. there is **there's**
4. are not **aren't**
5. we will **we'll**
6. were not **weren't**
7. I am **I'm**
8. did not **didn't**
9. you are **you're**
10. I shall **I'll**

> Use the contraction doesn't when referring to one person, place or thing.
> Use the contraction don't when referring to more than one and with the words I and you.
> He doesn't understand the direction.
> I don't know the way.

Cross out the incorrect word in parenthesis.

1. Our vacation (~~don't~~, doesn't) begin until tomorrow.
2. They (don't, ~~doesn't~~) expect to do much sightseeing.
3. She (~~don't~~, doesn't) have a camera to take pictures of her trip.
4. The shuttle bus to the plane (~~don't~~, doesn't) hold many people.
5. You (don't, ~~doesn't~~) have to hurry.
6. I (don't ~~doesn't~~) like to rush through the airport.
7. The noise of the jets (~~don't~~, doesn't) bother me.
8. (Don't, ~~Doesn't~~) worry about the baggage.
9. They hope the suitcases (don't, ~~doesn't~~) arrive until they have checked into customs.
10. That plane (doesn't, ~~don't~~) land at this airport.

Page 99

Page 100

Compound Words Name _____

> Some words are made by putting two words together. They form a compound word.
> water + melon = watermelon

Match a word from Column A with a word in Column B to make a compound word. Write the new word on the line below.

Column A		Column B	
1. box	9. play	road	ache
2. in	10. home	mate	work
3. ground	11. sail	ski	boat
4. rail	12. him	side	cock
5. pea	13. foot	loose	shine
6. soft	14. tooth	self	ball
7. sun	15. water	car	ride
8. water	16. over	ball	fall

1. **boxcar**
2. **inside**
3. **groundball**
4. **railroad**
5. **peacock**
6. **softball**
7. **sunshine**
8. **waterski**
9. **playmate**
10. **homework**
11. **sailboat**
12. **himself**
13. **footloose**
14. **toothache**
15. **waterfall**
16. **override**

ANT + EATER = ANTEATER

Page 100

Answer Key

Capital Letter Review Name _____

In the sentences below, circle the words that should begin with a capital letter.

(have) you been to (new) (orleans, louisiana?)

1. (louisiana) is a state in the (deep) (south)
2. (its) nickname is the (pelican) (state)
3. (some) refer to it as the nation's sugar bowl.
4. (louisiana) was named after (louis) XIV.
5. (he) was king of (france) nearly 300 years ago.
6. (louisiana) has many tourist attractions.
7. (creole) food is very good to eat.
8. (vieux) (carre) is the (french) (quarter)
9. (new) (orleans) is below sea level.
10. (baton) (rouge) is the capital.
11. (new) (orleans) is a popular city.
12. (mardi) (gras) is a special time.
13. (most) of the land is fertile.
14. (did) you know the (french) settled (louisiana?)
15. (they) were followed by the (spaniards)
16. (after) the (revolutionary) (war) (british) colonists settled there.
17. (most) people today are (american) born.
18. (french) customs and traditions remain alive.
19. (many) plantations are still in use.
20. (most) of the people in southern (louisiana) are (roman) (catholic)

Page 101

Punctuation Review Name _____

Put the correct form of punctuation in the following sentences.

Insects frighten me.

1. An insect is a small animal.
2. It is an invertebrate animal which means it has no spine.
3. Did you know every insect has three parts?
4. These parts are the head, thorax and abdomen.
5. Biting insects have strong jaws.
6. Insects pollinate flowers.
7. Do you like to catch insects?
8. The honeybee provides us with honey.
9. Wow! Silkworms spin thread.
10. How many insects are there?
11. More than 800,000 different species have been described.
12. Moths, butterflies, ants, bees, wasps and flies are just a few.
13. Some insects lay eggs.
14. Many produce in large numbers.
15. Are you allergic to bees?
16. Yes, I am.
17. I love to catch butterflies.
18. My bug collection is fantastic!
19. The word "bug" is a slang word.
20. Insects benefit us.

Page 102

About the book . . .

This book offers a wide variety of activities that provide a knowledge of the "rules and regulations" of proper English usage. Some of the basic skills addressed are: Parts of speech, plurals, verb tense, punctuation, sentences, possession, synonyms, antonyms, homonyms, etc.
Illustrated to enhance student motivation, these activities are packed with skill drills.

About the authors . . .

John Potter is an experienced teacher at the elementary level who has taught kindergarten through sixth grade. His belief in the emphasis on basic skills is the key to his success.

Having taught for thirteen years, **Carla Re Hirbe** is experienced in all areas on the elementary level. A graduate of Fontbonne College in St. Louis. her experience the last few years has been the teaching of language arts in a departmentalized program.

Author: John Potter/Carla Re Hirbe
Editor: Lee Quackenbush
Artists/Production: Jim Price/Carol Tiernon
Cover Art: Jan Vonk